W9-BLS-286

TO:

FROM:

DATE:

ADORED

365

DEVOTIONS FOR YOUNG WOMEN

ZONDERVAN®

ZONDERVAN

Adored

This title is also available as a Zondervan ebook.

Requests for information should be addressed to:
Zondervan, *3900 Sparks Dr. SE, Grand Rapids, Michigan 49546*

ISBN 978-0-310-76279-9

Published in association with the Books & Such Literary Management, 52 Mission Circle, Suite 122, PMB 170, Santa Rosa, California 95409-5370, www.booksandsuch.com

Content Contributor: Lindsay A. Franklin
Interior design: Denise Froehlich

Printed in the United States of America

18 19 20 21 22 23 24 25 /LSC/ 14 13 12 11 10 9 8 7 6 5 4 3

INTRODUCTION

Love is such a complicated word for so few letters. We might say we love a lot of different things—our friends, close family members, mentors . . . or the book we just read, a chai tea latte, and chocolate-chip cookies. The word *love* means something different in each of those contexts, doesn't it? Throw in the love found in romantic relationships, and we have a full spectrum of complex feelings. And all expressed using those four little letters.

Maybe the fact that this little word has so many different uses is the reason we struggle to understand what it really means when the Bible tells us God loves us. Not only does God love us, but he himself *is* love. We can figure out pretty quickly we're talking about something other than chocolate-chip-cookie love, but that doesn't necessarily help us understand what God does mean when he says he loves us.

The fact is, God doesn't just love us. He adores us. And maybe we struggle to understand that because we look in the mirror and wonder why the great big God of the Universe would look at us and think, "Yes. *She* is my adored, beloved daughter." But make no mistake: no matter what our insecurities try to tell us, God does delight in us, his beautiful creations. This devotional will explore God's great love for us. We'll look at everything from deep spiritual truths to the everyday ups and downs of life.

There's a short scripture verse and devotional message for every day of the year, but you don't have to start at the beginning of the year *or* the book! Start where you like. Read as many as you like. One per day is great, but the important thing is that you keep going, keep learning more about our amazing God and his limitless love. And if his Spirit moves you, let God know how much *you* adore *him* on the journaling lines following each devotion ...

All right, adored daughter. Let's get started.

DAY 1

"But God demonstrates his own love for us in this: While we were still sinners, Christ died for us."

—ROMANS 5:8

We are God's adored. *You* are his cherished, treasured possession. That's a tough truth to swallow sometimes. When we feel awkward, rejected, misunderstood, or lonely, it's hard to imagine the God of the universe even remembers us, let alone adores us. And who isn't awkward ninety-seven percent of the time? Ninety-nine if you count the times we run into things, trip over our own feet, or drop things just because.

But it's true. God does adore us. His very character reveals to us just how deeply we're loved. This God—this unchangeable, eternal, beautiful, jealous, all-knowing, all-powerful, merciful God of love—knows you by name. He calls you his own, and, despite his utter bigness, he sent his son into the world to save you long before you were ever born. That's how much he adores you. And by getting to know him in all his glory, we learn exactly how big a deal it is to be called "adored."

> *"[The foundations of the earth] will perish, but you remain; they will all wear out like a garment. Like clothing you will change them and they will be discarded. But you remain the same, and your years will never end."*
>
> —PSALM 102:26–27

Maybe you've never thought much about God remaining the same, always and forever. Sure, you've seen the Bible verses that say God is the same yesterday, today, and forever. But have you ever thought about why that's so important, or how much it affects your life?

Can you imagine if God was changeable? What if his standards, his nature, his very *self* evolved the way our culture does? What if what God thought was acceptable one second was the next second deemed uncool, unwise, or flat-out wrong? Even worse, what if the greatest gift God has ever given to you was suddenly taken back because God changed his mind?

But he never will. God is unchangeable. He remains the same, always. What he promised yesterday still stands today. He sent his son to the cross because you are so loved. Your redemption was worth it to God—and he hasn't changed his mind.

DAY 3

"In the beginning God created the heavens and the earth."

—GENESIS 1:1

It would be cliché to start our devotions with the first verse of the Bible. So we're doing it on Day 3. Because we're original like that.

There's this indescribably huge, massively powerful, amazingly creative God who made everything. I bet you've read that before—like if you've sat in any Sunday school class, ever. So when you feel the warmth of the sun on your face, see the beauty of a natural landscape, study the intricacy of a human cell, you know God made all that. He spoke, and it was. He imagined, and it was born. Every good thing you see, taste, hear, touch, think, or feel is a result of that God-creation.

And this is the same God who wants to hear about your day. This is the same God who tells you to come to him when you're tired, overloaded, stressed-out. This is the same God who tells you to pray to him, ask for good things, trust him with your hopes and fears. Do you think he's able to hold those details in the palm of his universe-sized hand? Of course. Because your God is the God of the beginning.

DAY 4

"Jesus Christ is the same yesterday and today and forever."

—HEBREWS 13:8

Pop culture changes by the second. The new It-Couple breaks up and makes up faster than the paparazzi can snap the pics to prove it. Social media moves at warp speed. If you blink, you've missed the latest hashtag or filter. It's impossible to stay on top of it all. And we may very well decide we have no desire to!

When much of our culture is strapped to an ever-changing merry-go-round of reality TV and rising and falling stars, it's difficult to fathom someone who stays the same. Forever. Since always. But that's what we have in Jesus. Our savior isn't sweating to keep up with anyone, and he's not struggling to conquer the latest social media craze. He's constant and unchanging in a world that never slows down, never stands still. No matter what else is shifting in your life, you can trust in the steadfastness of Christ.

"Every good and perfect gift is from above, coming down from the Father of the heavenly lights, who does not change like shifting shadows."

—JAMES 1:17

"You do you." Ever heard anyone say that? It sounds simple, but it's not always easy to "do you" when there's pressure to conform to what everyone else is doing. For you, that pressure may feel most intense at school, on the sports field, at church, or at home. No matter where you go, there will always be people who expect you to act, think, or even dress in a certain way.

It's not always a bad thing to fit in with the crowd. But what about conforming when it would compromise who you are or, worse, your beliefs? That's a no-go. Your personal identity and your identity in Christ are two priceless gifts from God. Protect them. Stand firm in who you are, knowing God is always true to himself, and we can be, too. You do you.

"Do you not know that your bodies are temples of the Holy Spirit, who is in you, whom you have received from God? You are not your own; you were bought at a price. Therefore honor God with your bodies."

—1 CORINTHIANS 6:19–20

Anyone remember the Great Yoga Pants War of 2014? Everyone had an opinion on modesty—bare shoulders are scandalous, girls shouldn't wear spandex when working out, skinny jeans should be banned, let's nix shorts while we're at it. And let us not even speak of midriffs or bathing suits.

So, is there truth in the chatter? The Bible doesn't give us two lists of clothing, one forbidden and one acceptable. No one can tell you precisely how God feels about wearing leggings as pants. But we do know that the same God who inspired 1 Corinthians 6:19–20 is the Lord of our lives. And so we know God wants us to treat our bodies with respect, and that includes not reducing our beautiful, wonderful bodies to objects.

The greatest danger in failing to respect our bodies in this way is that we, God's adored daughters, begin to believe our worth lies in our physical beauty or sexual attractiveness. You are more than your sex appeal, beloved daughter. Honor your worth.

DAY 7

"God is not human, that he should lie, not a human being, that he should change his mind. Does he speak and then not act? Does he promise and not fulfill?"

—NUMBERS 23:19

Have you ever broken a promise to anyone? Said you'd do something then failed to follow through? Yeah, me neither . . . ahem.

God makes a lot of promises in the Bible. He makes promises to the Israelites, promises to the church, promises to those who love him. Those promises can feel distant when you read them—like they're just words written on scrolls thousands of years ago that have nothing to do with your life today. Nothing to do with us. Except . . . wait. Are you part of the church? Do you love God? Does that mean—can it mean—those promises are really for you, today? Right here, as you read this book, maybe in your pajamas?

Yes! The truth is, even though those promises are over two thousand years old, God hasn't gone back on his word. How do we know? Because to do so would be to deny his own unchangeable essence. He doesn't change. He doesn't break his word. So drink in those promises. They're for you.

DAY 8

"And my God will meet all your needs according to the riches of his glory in Christ Jesus."

—PHILIPPIANS 4:19

There's another God-promise here. Needs met in riches. So, that means you can upgrade your Civic to a Bentley or, even better, a vintage Mustang. Right? You can expect a brand-new wardrobe. Or you get unlimited shopping sprees at your local bookstore, electronics store, shoe store, or office supply store? (Hey, not judging . . .)

Not exactly. The apostle Paul was telling the Philippians that God would meet all their needs, as they'd been so generous to Paul and mindful of his needs. So what's the unchangeable promise here for *us*? Give with an open hand, and our God will return our faithfulness with *his* generosity. God is capable of greater generosity than we can imagine, let alone practice, and his generosity isn't limited to—or even focused on—material things. Is our every want going to be fulfilled? Only if that's what's truly best for us—and usually, it's not. Our faithful, unchangeable God always sees the big picture and brings about what's ultimately best for his children.

DAY 9

"I lift up my eyes to the mountains—where does my help come from? My help comes from the LORD, the Maker of heaven and earth."

—PSALM 121:1–2

There are so many promises in the Bible to cling to, especially when we're down, alone, hard-pressed, and feeling like nothing is going right. (Read David's psalms for proof!) And sometimes "cling" is truly the word. The image is perfect—holding on for dear life, barely hanging in, white-knuckled and eyes squeezed shut, waiting for the raging storm to blow over. Ever been there?

Remembering God through the dark times isn't always easy. When our fingers are digging into the rocky face of life's struggles, perhaps God and his good promises aren't the first things that pop to mind. But those moments are the absolute perfect times to lean on God's promises. He promises never to leave. He promises to take care of our needs. And he promises salvation to all who have faith in his son, Jesus.

Are you weathering a storm right now? If so, you're in good company. Rest in the promises of God. Our help comes from him, maker of heaven and earth.

DAY 10

"No, in all these things we are more than conquerors through him who loved us."

—ROMANS 8:37

Romans 8:37 is such a great verse. More than conquerors—what an image! It's not just an image of Christians being victorious. It's an image of Christians being super-victorious. Uber-conquerors. Ultra-winners.

But what are "these things" we're more than conquerors over through Christ? We have to back up a couple verses to find out, but the short list is: trouble, hardship, persecution, famine, nakedness, danger, or sword—things that would seek to separate us from the love of Christ. Does the verse promise we'll never experience hardship? Sadly, no. Instead, the verse promises we will persevere through such things and never be separated from the love of Christ. We're ultra-winners over anything seeking to detach us from our faith. God promises that no matter what troubles you experience in life, you have already been granted true victory over them.

DAY 11

"Therefore, my dear brothers and sisters, stand firm. Let nothing move you. Always give yourselves fully to the work of the Lord, because you know that your labor in the Lord is not in vain."

—1 CORINTHIANS 15:58

In many ways, the modern world values consistency. Healthy eating, regular exercise, excellent school and work attendance, faithfully doing your chores (ugh, do I have to?)—these are important, if mundane, ways we're encouraged to show consistency.

Is that a challenge for you? Are you free-spirited, skeptical of plans, schedules, and routines? Or do you thrive on the day-in, day-out sameness and neatness of a consistent routine? Do you land somewhere in the middle?

No matter how you're built, striving for consistency is a godly goal. We want to be people who follow through—those who are dependable and who stand firm, giving ourselves fully to our work. When we do, we reflect our steadfast God of order who delights in the small things. You may never love folding that mountain of clean laundry sitting on your bed or doing the dishes every day, but you can find joy in a strong work ethic and the relaxation that comes after a job well done.

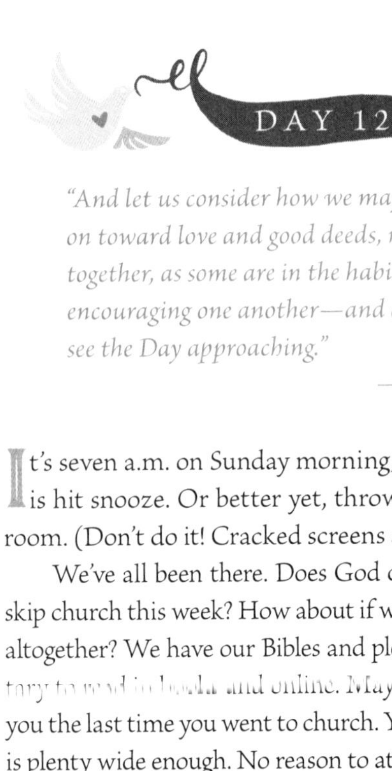

DAY 12

"And let us consider how we may spur one another on toward love and good deeds, not giving up meeting together, as some are in the habit of doing, but encouraging one another—and all the more as you see the Day approaching."

—HEBREWS 10:24–25

It's seven a.m. on Sunday morning, and all you want to do is hit snooze. Or better yet, throw your phone across the room. (Don't do it! Cracked screens are sad.)

We've all been there. Does God care if we hit snooze and skip church this week? How about if we give up going to church altogether? We have our Bibles and plenty of biblical commentary to read in books and online. Maybe no one even looked at you the last time you went to church. Your social circle at school is plenty wide enough. No reason to attend church . . . right?

Except the Bible encourages regular gatherings amongst believers. Why? Being surrounded by other believers must be important. More mature believers can help you grow and answer tough questions for you. Less mature believers need people like you to look up to.

When we're surrounded by other believers, we're united by a common purpose, and that purpose is to glorify God. If you feel disconnected at church, find somewhere to serve. Find someone to mentor. Ask someone to mentor you. Just don't hit snooze every week. The church needs you—and you need it.

DAY 13

"Whoever can be trusted with very little can also be trusted with much, and whoever is dishonest with very little will also be dishonest with much."

—LUKE 16:10

You know what being faithful, honest, and trustworthy with small tasks gets you? Larger tasks. It sounds like more work, doesn't it? Sometimes it is. But think of it this way—those larger tasks are like a job promotion.

Most job promotions come with a greater level of responsibility, and that might mean more or harder work. But it also means greater pay. Depending on the job, it can mean better hours, more respect, a cooler title, a better uniform . . . especially when you're starting at the bottom of the ladder and your uniform may include frumpy pants and a hideous foam visor.

So while faithfulness with small tasks may result in larger tasks and more work, God sees and honors our faithfulness. He blesses that faithfulness. This blessing might not come in the worldly sense—money, better titles, less hideous uniforms—but it'll come. God's designs are often bigger than we guess.

DAY 14

"Because God wanted to make the unchanging nature of his purpose very clear to the heirs of what was promised, he confirmed it with an oath. God did this so that, by two unchangeable things in which it is impossible for God to lie, we who have fled to take hold of the hope set before us may be greatly encouraged."

—HEBREWS 6:17–18

Do you ever look around at your life and wonder, how did I get here? Sometimes that's a positive question. We see all the rich blessings of our lives, and we're overwhelmed by God's goodness. Other times, we see one giant mess of hurt, anxiety, disappointment, disaster—or even neglect or abuse.

Even if you have experienced the latter, these words are still for you: God is at work in your life. He's watching, involved, engaged in your life when you're at school and when you're at home. He's with you whether you're feeling happy or sad, frustrated or thrilled. He's at work in your life when everything is sailing along just as you hoped it would, and he's at work in your life when it seems like nothing is going right.

That's because his purpose, since the beginning of his dealings with mankind, hasn't changed. And that purpose is to bring his adored children back to himself. He's working to that end this very second, whether our circumstances are the result of God's abundant mercy or the sin of this fallen world. He is there, and he's drawing you close, adored one.

DAY 15

"But Ruth replied, 'Don't urge me to leave you or to turn back from you. Where you go I will go, and where you stay I will stay. Your people will be my people and your God my God. Where you die I will die, and there I will be buried. May the Lord *deal with me, be it ever so severely, if even death separates you and me.'"*

—RUTH 1:16–17

Ruth was a Moabite married to an Israelite. After her husband died, Ruth insisted on returning to Israel with her widowed mother-in-law. This is pretty incredible, guys. Moab was one of the idolatrous nations the Israelites were supposed to destroy. Moab is only spoken of as a cursed, rejected people. And yet here is a young Moabite woman determined to accept the Israelite God as her own. It's nothing short of a miracle.

So what happens to Ruth? She marries an upstanding Israelite man named Boaz. They have children, and Ruth eventually becomes King David's grandmother. Which means she's included in the genealogy of Jesus. This woman, from a cursed people, is part of the Hebrew savior's lineage.

In Ruth's time, bloodlines mattered. She wasn't part of the chosen nation, but God drew Ruth to himself and called her *adored*. He honored her faith, even though she didn't seem to fit the mold of "God's chosen" at the time. If you've ever felt like an outsider, be encouraged. Ruth's story proves God has always had a heart for the outsider—and he always will.

DAY 16

"For you created my inmost being; you knit me together in my mother's womb."

—PSALM 139:13

Have you ever seen ultrasound pictures of yourself? Those grainy, black-and-white images likely made your parents squeal, cry tears of joy, or stare in wonder. Maybe all of the above.

Even if you haven't seen ultrasound pictures of yourself, you probably have a good idea what they look like. Tiny humans at eight weeks gestation look something like lima beans with heartbeats. Glorious little miracles.

And yet, even before you were a lima bean with a heartbeat, God knew you. In fact, he pieced together that lima bean person from a couple of cells. He knew what you'd look like, which traits you'd pull from which chromosomes and how all those traits would come together to create you. He knew what tiny temperament he'd infuse into that little brain and heart. He assembled all the parts, and then—whoosh—breath of God, breath of life. Like magic, there's the girl he knew before she even was. God has known you, always.

DAY 17

"Be strong and courageous. Do not fear or be in dread of them, for it is the Lord *your God who goes with you. He will not leave you or forsake you."*

—DEUTERONOMY 31:6

It's hard to grasp the constancy of God because we're fickle. All of us. Sure, people are fickle to varying degrees. Every human lands somewhere on the fickleness scale, from butterfly to tortoise. Butterflies are the flighty free spirits who zip around life, smelling roses, taking in the moment, only landing in one spot for a split second. Tortoises lumber along—slowly, surely—not getting anywhere quickly, perhaps, but through determination and focus, they're bound to arrive at their destination eventually.

But even the most plodding tortoise of us all is flighty compared to God. We're self-focused, which is a nicer way of saying self-centered. We tend to switch course when some greener grass sprouts up somewhere. But God doesn't work that way.

Our God—the one of unchanging purpose, constant love, utmost consistency—never discovers greener grass and decides to graze over there for a bit. He knows all the grass. He's not wooed by the bigger, better deal. He's not suddenly walking alongside you in life, only to be distracted, shout "Squirrel!" and take off after it.

God won't give up on you. He won't forget you. He won't leave you. Ever.

DAY 18

"And I tell you that you are Peter, and on this rock I will build my church, and the gates of Hades will not overcome it."

—MATTHEW 16:18

Have you had an experience with a bully? You're definitely not alone. Most people know what it's like to be picked on, and some of us know what it's like to be physically or emotionally attacked by those who seem intent on tearing us down. If you're in that situation now, don't be afraid to get whatever help you need. Talk to someone you trust.

Dealing with a bully can definitely make you feel like you're standing at the gates of Hades, which is the Greek word for hell. But you don't have to live in fear.

You have a God who offers peace. You have a God who hears your prayers. You have a God who never backs down, even from the very gates of hell. You are *never* alone and your God is *never* overcome. So stand tall. You can trust God to help you overcome those who are trying to intimidate you.

DAY 19

"He raises the poor from the dust and lifts the needy from the ash heap; he seats them with princes and has them inherit a throne of honor."

—1 SAMUEL 2:8

You know what's even more complicated than being bullied yourself? Watching it happen to someone else. You know it's wrong. You know you should say something—stand up for the person being picked on. But if you do, you risk turning the bully's focus onto you. And so your fight-or-flight reflex says, "Run! It's not worth it! Too much danger!"

But we know that God's heart is with the oppressed—the person in the dust, the needy one in the ash heap. And if God's heart is there, shouldn't ours be too?

So what can you do if you're not in a position to physically step in for someone? You can certainly get the help of someone who is in a position of authority. Many school campuses, in particular, have zero-tolerance policies on bullying. You can also meet the bullied person in her ash heap. Let her know she's not alone. Let her know you haven't forgotten her—that someone cares. Let her see God's love through you.

"Jesus wept."

—JOHN 11:35

"The feels." Do you ever feel swallowed by your emotions? Pressed down, overwhelmed, shredded—like you're drowning? Everyone has been there at least once, and some of us find ourselves there a lot.

It can make us feel small and a little crazy to be overwhelmed by our feelings. Sometimes we might even feel pressure to pretend everything is okay—to put on a happy face, a perfect veneer with no weakness, no broken spots, no cracks marring the surface. To seem perfect, even when we're falling apart.

That's why we have verses in the Bible like this one. Those two words—Jesus wept—are so powerful. Jesus was grieving the loss of his friend, Lazarus. He mourned. He felt. And he wept. The Bible doesn't say, "And Jesus recited the perfect verse from the Scriptures and told the people to pray harder, then serenely glided home." Jesus. Wept. We have a savior who knows about the feels—a savior who *felt* the feels—and though he shed those tears over two thousand years ago, he hasn't forgotten. He hasn't changed. He weeps with the brokenhearted.

DAY 21

"Wait for the Lord; be strong and take heart and wait for the Lord."

—PSALM 27:14

Have you ever heard that old joke that you should pray for patience, or else God will give you opportunities to practice it?

Most of us don't find waiting easy. When we have a craving for something delicious, we want it *now,* not after dinner. (Ice cream for breakfast? Sure, why not!) When we have a fun event on the horizon, we want the horizon to be *here,* already. When we have a dream or goal, we want it realized *immediately.* Today. Yesterday, even. Let's get this show on the road! What are we waiting for?!

But given how much Scripture talks about waiting, specifically waiting on the Lord, we can guess patience is listed as fruit of the Spirit for a reason. God is never in a rush. This God who is always the same says, "Wait on me. See what I have for you in *my* time." And here's a secret: God's plan in God's time is always even better than ice cream for breakfast. God's not in a rush, so why are we?

DAY 22

"You have heard that it was said, 'Love your neighbor and hate your enemy.' But I tell you, love your enemies and pray for those who persecute you, that you may be children of your Father in heaven. He causes his sun to rise on the evil and the good, and sends rain on the righteous and the unrighteous."

—MATTHEW 5:43–45

What did that verse just say? Love our enemies? Impossible! At least it feels that way. And yet here's Jesus, telling us the standard for his followers. We want to cry out, "But Jesus! The enemies of my life, my family, my church, my country, my world are bigger and badder than the people you were speaking to way back then!"

But Jesus didn't give exceptions, caveats, or exclusions. Jesus said it simply. Love your enemies, pray for your persecutors, and let God serve as their judge. Want another crazy truth? Those enemies of ours are human beings, loved by God. No matter how much we want to lump people into categories of good and bad, the Bible shows us that God loves all people and wants all people to return to him. How can they if the people of God don't share the love of God with everyone?

What are some practical ways you can love your enemies? Pray for them. Pray for your own heart to be softened toward them. And most importantly, forgive them with the bigness of the forgiveness we've received in Christ.

DAY 23

"But I trust in your unfailing love; my heart rejoices in your salvation."

—PSALM 13:15

God's unfailing love. Have you ever heard that expression before? *Unfailing.* Can you imagine never failing at something? How about never failing to love? It's hard to love the unlovable. Being real, sometimes it's hard to love the people we *do* love!

Sadly, we won't get to experience what it's like to be unfailing on this side of eternity. We make mistakes. We mess up. We disappoint. We sin. But that's why God's unfailing love is so important, so necessary. It's vitally necessary to our salvation that his love never fails . . . because we fail so often. Our unfaithfulness is met with his faithfulness. Our error is met with his righteousness. Our indifference is met by the endless ocean of his love.

Today, let's rejoice in our salvation, borne from a love that never fails.

DAY 24

"For Ezra had devoted himself to the study and observance of the Law of the Lord, and to teaching its decrees and laws in Israel."

—EZRA 7:10

Ezra gets a really cool one-liner—the one-sentence description that sums up who he was and what he did. Devoted to the study and observance of the Law. Wow! That's a one-liner rooted in faithfulness and consistency.

Have you ever thought about what your one-liner would be? "Went to school, watched TV, ate stuff." Or how about, "Got decent grades, went to church, fought with siblings, won most of the time." Maybe, "Wrote words, most of them stank." These are probably the one-liners of our nightmares.

But what about your ideal one-liner? If you could have your life summed up in one line, what would you like that one line to be? What if you thought about that one line every time you got up in the morning? Or how about every time you opened your mouth to say something? (Eep!) Maybe you're not sure who you are or who you'd like to be yet. That's okay. Here's a one-liner we can all claim: adored daughter of God learning to grow in his love. Own it!

DAY 25

"How priceless is your unfailing love, O God! People take refuge in the shadow of your wings."

—PSALM 36:7

We throw around the word "love" a lot. We love a certain time of year, a certain outfit, a cool band, a favorite store, a favorite book, a class, a teacher, our new phone. On a deeper level, we love our friends, our parents, our siblings, our other family members.

It's not a bad thing to express positive feelings about the wonderful things that make us happy, and it's absolutely correct to love the special people God has placed in our lives. But if we say "love" so often it becomes ordinary, do we dilute our understanding of God's love? Do we lose sight of what his love is like when we think of God loving us the way we "love" our half-syrup mocha with extra whip?

God's love isn't a passing fancy or a strong like. God's love is not a taste preference. God's love isn't a crush. God's love is a since-the-beginning-of-time sacrifice. God's love is a rip-out-your-heart, bleed-in-the-street-for-you love. God's love is a never-disappearing promise.

DAY 26

"When I was a child, I talked like a child, I thought like a child, I reasoned like a child. When I became a man, I put the ways of childhood behind me."

—1 CORINTHIANS 13:11

Be who you are. Whether you're quiet, outgoing, adventure-seeking, a homebody, athletic, studious, artsy, a talker, a listener, a thinker, a feeler, or some glorious combination of the above, God made you *you*, and you're beautiful. Embrace it!

But does being who you are mean that, like God, you should be unchangeable—that you should always stay the same? We've looked at ways we can reflect God's unchangeableness—by being consistent, steadfast, trustworthy, dependable, and patient. But the Bible shows us ways we *should* change. Unlike God, we're not sinless. We have challenges to overcome, deficiencies that hold us back, cause us to mess up, and keep us from the fullest life God has for us.

We can embrace our unique selves while changing in the ways God wants us to. God wants us to continually grow in spiritual and emotional maturity. No matter how old you are, there's always room for further growth in Christ, and that's the kind of changing God desires from us.

DAY 27

"We ought always to thank God for you, brothers and sisters, and rightly so, because your faith is growing more and more, and the love all of you have for one another is increasing."

—2 THESSALONIANS 1:3

Faith isn't static. It's not a one-time event you experience, then set aside. Faith is dynamic. It moves, grows, deepens. As we walk beside Jesus, one step at a time, our faith in who he is and what he promises expands and sharpens.

Notice we didn't say "one *day* at a time"? That's because, while faith is dynamic (changing and growing), it isn't always linear (in a straight line). You may hear people describe youth camp or mission trips as "mountaintop experiences." That's because those cool, special events are like exciting peaks in our walks with Jesus. But the opposite exists in our walks too. We call them "valley seasons."

Sometimes we feel far from God. Not only does our faith not seem to be growing, it feels like it's shrinking. We've gone full-Grinch, and our hearts are two sizes too small. Don't worry. It doesn't mean you've lost your faith. You're just going through a valley season, and the only way to get through a valley is to keep walking. One step at a time. On the other side of that valley is deeper faith, a closer God, a more personal Jesus.

DAY 28

". . . so that you may live a life worthy of the Lord and please him in every way: bearing fruit in every good work, growing in the knowledge of God . . ."

—COLOSSIANS 1:10

A life worthy of the Lord that pleases him in every way? Oh, sure. No problem. Piece of cake. What's the next challenge?

Ahem.

These verses can seem really daunting. A life "worthy of the Lord" seems impossible when we consider the insides of our hearts—all the gross spots we'd rather hide from the world. And you know who sees all those spots and the ones we haven't even found yet? God. How can we possibly live our entire lives to please him? Can we just breeze past these verses and skip to some that tell us God loves us just where we're at?

The truth is, we can't breeze past this stuff. One area God absolutely commands us to continue growing in is holiness. So, what does that mean? It means we walk ever-closer to God's standard. We love better, flee from sin faster, run harder toward our faith. What is one thing—just one—you could change about your thoughts, words, or actions that would bring greater holiness to your life? Do it. And then find another. And then another. Pray that God would help you in each of these little steps. That's how we grow in holiness and live a life worthy of the Lord.

DAY 29

"And this is my prayer: that your love may abound more and more in knowledge and depth of insight . . ."

—PHILIPPIANS 1:9

Abound—flourish, prosper, overflow. Our love is to overflow in increasing measure as we grow closer to Jesus. Think of Jesus-love as a continual laying down of self—meaning love is a choice to put another person before yourself. A sacrifice.

On day one of being a Christian, how good were you at putting someone else's needs before your own? "Overflowing" may not be the word you would use to describe your day-one level of love. Maybe a trickle was more like it. Our sinful nature makes us selfish—concerned for our own survival, our own needs, our own comfort. Once we accept Jesus, the Holy Spirit helps us break free from our selfish sinful behaviors. The Spirit helps us learn to love the way Jesus did.

Have you grown in love since day one of being a Christian? Are you abounding in love yet—overflowing, spilling it from your heart and mouth? Think of some concrete ways you can show sacrificial love to others today.

DAY 30

"Do not let your hearts be troubled. You believe in God; believe also in me. My Father's house has many rooms; if that were not so, would I have told you that I am going there to prepare a place for you? And if I go and prepare a place for you, I will come back and take you to be with me that you also may be where I am."

—JOHN 14:1–3

Jesus has prepared a place for us. And he's coming back to take us with him. He said so, and we know he doesn't change his promises.

That means before you were able to understand Jesus or a single word of the Bible, Jesus had prepared your place beside him. Just think about that for a second. Jesus made a place for you.

Exactly how adored do you think a person must be to have Jesus, Son of God, prepare a place for her? And it's not a temporary place that might last for a moment, then disappear. It's not something he'll snatch back, change his mind about, or forget about. He prepared a place for each of us in eternity. That means the rest of time, stretching on forever. You, adored daughter, will dwell forever with him in the Heavenly Temple. Rejoice!

"If our hearts condemn us, we know that God is greater than our hearts, and he knows everything."

—1 JOHN 3:20

He knows everything. Sometimes we hear this truth described in big theological terms—God's omniscience—but it's really a very simple truth, just like John says it. God knows everything.

God is never shocked. He isn't surprised by natural disasters or current events we may find terrifying. He isn't confused by the way sin continues to affect our world or any given person's life. He isn't stymied by humanity's unfaithfulness, the straying of his adored children, or the catastrophes we don't see coming, whether on a global scale or in our own lives.

He *knows everything.* Every struggle of every people group, the problems of every nation, the depths of every single heart—including yours. And still he walks beside you, offers his love, and promises never to abandon you. You are not just loved. You are *known* and loved.

DAY 32

"To God belong wisdom and power; counsel and understanding are his."

—JOB 12:13

God's mind goes deeper than his knowledge. He doesn't just know every nook and cranny of everything, everywhere. God also possesses perfect wisdom.

So what's the difference between knowledge and wisdom? Knowledge is about facts. God knows all things actual and possible—that's his omniscient knowledge. But wisdom is about the application of knowledge. Not only does God know all the facts, but he has chosen the best plan, the best goals, and the best ways to achieve those goals.

If this feels a bit like Big Truth that has nothing to do with real life, keep reading. God's wisdom means you, adored daughter of God, can trust in him. You can trust in his plan for the world and his plan for your life. You can—and should—rely on God's wisdom because his wise plans, based on his perfect knowledge, are always the best.

DAY 33

"Naaman's servants went to him and said, 'My father, if the prophet had told you to do some great thing, would you not have done it? How much more, then, when he tells you, "Wash and be cleansed"!'"

—2 KINGS 5:13

Isn't it weird how sometimes it's easier to do the big things God asks of us? If God boomed from heaven, "You! Go to the ends of the earth to reach people who have never heard my name!" we might find that easier than if he simply whispered to our hearts, "Psst. I want you to talk about Jesus to your next-door neighbor."

Naaman had this complex. He was a well-respected foreign commander who had leprosy, which was a big deal in the days before antibiotics. He sought healing from the Israelite prophet Elisha, but instead of the showy production he expected from the famous prophet, Elisha sent a messenger (how rude!) to tell him to bathe in the Jordan River and he'd be healed. Naaman was furious. The Jordan, even in those days, was pretty muddy and gross. Really, Naaman was being asked to humble himself and trust God's plan.

Good news for him, he eventually did. His servants convinced him to reconsider, and he was healed. What can we learn from Naaman's story? Whether the tasks God gives us are great or small, showy or humble, we can always trust in his wise plan.

"Abram believed the Lord, and he credited it to him as righteousness."

—GENESIS 15:6

Abraham trusted in God's good plan—in God's perfect wisdom—when facing the impossible. Even the casual student of biology will understand it's pretty impossible to get pregnant when you're ninety years old. But Abraham's wife was ninety years old when God said she would get pregnant and have a long-promised child. And Abraham believed him. Faced with the impossible—even the ridiculous—Abraham trusted God's wisdom.

Is there a situation in your life that seems hopeless right now? Maybe there's a class you're struggling in, or you're having problems with friends. Maybe you're getting bullied online or your parents are splitting up. When you feel like you're facing the impossible, you can rest in God's perfect wisdom. Things don't always work out exactly the way we want them to, but we can lean on the knowledge that God hasn't forgotten about us, and he's still working his plan. God knows the details of your situation. The "impossible" has never thwarted his plan before. Trust it.

DAY 35

"As the heavens are higher than the earth, so are my ways higher than your ways and my thoughts than your thoughts."

—ISAIAH 55:9

Trusting God when we're walking through daily life is hard enough. Trusting God in the face of impossible circumstances, like Abraham, is even harder. But trusting God through those times when everything feels like it's falling apart is the hardest of all.

Have you been there before? All of us either have or will be one day. We experience circumstances that are straight-up terrible. Pain, loss, destruction, confusion. Does it mean God's plan is falling apart? Does it mean we can't trust him anymore?

Quite the opposite, actually. During those hardest times, we have words like Isaiah's to hold onto. God's ways are higher than ours. When we don't understand why life has become hard, even unbearable, trusting in God's wisdom frees our hearts to grow in our faith and endure the difficulty. Sometimes we have to endure for a short while, and sometimes it's months or years. But we can rest in the knowledge that God hasn't left us and he's working about his ultimate good plan because he loves us.

"And we know that in all things God works for the good of those who love him, who have been called according to his purpose."

—ROMANS 8:28

Great, God has a plan. But what in the world is that plan?! God does have a plan for your individual life. Remember, he knows everything—all the facts, and all the possibilities. But it can be hard to discern God's plan for our lives because there isn't a script in the Bible for every move we're supposed to make. There isn't a step-by-step guide to who you should be friends with, which college or career you should pursue, where you should live, who to marry, if you will have children. Wouldn't it simplify things if there were?

But the Bible *does* tell us many of God's big-picture plans, thankfully. God's ultimate plan is to save us and to make us more like Jesus. When we keep this in view, those smaller, daily decisions about our lives come into clearer focus. Does this choice help me live and love like Jesus? Or does it take me in the opposite direction? When we move forward like this, one step at a time, honoring God with each decision, his plan for our life unfolds.

DAY 37

"Search me, God, and know my heart; test me and know my anxious thoughts. See if there is any offensive way in me, and lead me in the way everlasting."

—PSALM 139:23–24

How do we get more of God's guidance in our lives? The answer is probably not one we want to hear. Are you ready anyway? Okay, here goes . . .

We ask God to search us, to take a good, hard look at our hearts. And then—*gulp*—we have to be willing to change. The phrase "any offensive way in me" doesn't leave a lot of room for "Hey, I know I'm sinning, but I *really* don't want to stop." If we're not careful, sin wraps around us like a warm blanket. So comfortable, so familiar. So hard to give up. But if we want more of God's leadership, we have to be willing to do the hard work of heart clean-up. That's how we keep growing, and that's how we see clearly enough to follow God as he leads us in the right direction.

What can you clean from your life or your heart today that will help you be open to God's plan for your life?

DAY 38

"So whether you eat or drink or whatever you do, do it all for the glory of God."

—1 CORINTHIANS 10:31

Every choice we make matters. There are real-world consequences for each decision in our lives—some of them good, some of them bad. Everything we do is like a stone tossed into a pond—we never know what sort of ripples it might make.

This thought can be overwhelming. We can become frozen in indecision, terrified of making the "wrong" choice. But God doesn't want us to live in fear. Instead, he wants us to make choices with wisdom. But how? First, does God's word teach against one of the options? If so, let's close that door right away because we know it's not God's plan for us. Of the remaining choices, do any help you live more like Jesus? Do any make you less like him? If so, head toward Jesus, not away from him.

What about the remaining options? Choose whichever seems most practical, most interesting, or best to you, and you're honoring God in your choices. No matter what we do, life will be a mix of good and bad for all of us because our world is not perfect. But we can honor God in our choices.

DAY 39

"Therefore, in order to keep me from becoming conceited, I was given a thorn in my flesh, a messenger of Satan, to torment me. Three times I pleaded with the Lord to take it away from me. But he said to me, 'My grace is sufficient for you, for my power is made perfect in weakness.'"

—2 CORINTHIANS 12:7B–9A

Thorns come in all shapes and sizes. Maybe it's a physical or emotional condition. Maybe it's a person in your life who seems bent on tearing you down.

Whatever form our "thorns" take, we can follow Paul's example here. First, it's okay to be frustrated. Paul's frustration can be seen in some of his words here: torment, pleaded. He wasn't happy about this situation. We can cry out to God when we're suffering.

Second, we see persistence in prayer. Paul prayed three times for this specific sickness, whatever it was.

But this story also shows us how to respond when God doesn't intervene. Paul accepted that God's ultimate plan—to make Paul more like Christ—was in motion and that God could be glorified in Paul's suffering. Paul even got some perspective on *why* God allowed this to happen. "To keep me from becoming conceited." God is always working his ultimate plan in our lives, even and especially when we're suffering.

DAY 40

"Therefore I will boast all the more gladly about my weaknesses, so that Christ's power may rest on me. That is why, for Christ's sake, I delight in weaknesses, in insults, in hardships, in persecutions, in difficulties. For when I am weak, then I am strong."

—2 CORINTHIANS 12:9B–10

When we're dealing with difficulties, sometimes it's hard to feel like God has a good, wise plan in the works. We want to tell God, "That's enough, now. You're all-powerful, so please take this away. Today. Actually, yesterday, if you don't mind."

But these verses tell a different story. When we are at our weakest and most broken—that's when Jesus is most clearly seen through us.

Think about it this way. You're like a clay jar with a light inside—the Holy Spirit living inside you. That light shines out of the top, maybe even overflows, when you are experiencing abundant blessings and excellent circumstances. But when that jar is cracked, that's when the light is shining most directly to the outside world. When we're experiencing hardship and, through the strength of the Holy Spirit, we're *still* able to practice patience and peace, to experience joy, to show love to others . . . that's when Jesus's love shines through the broken spots and touches the broken spots in other people.

Like Paul, we can rejoice in our weakness as it reveals Christ's strength.

DAY 41

"For the LORD gives wisdom; from his mouth come knowledge and understanding."

—PROVERBS 2:6

Some of God's traits have no direct connection to our human experience. Omnipresence, for example. Being all places at all times is just a tad outside anything we can relate to.

But wisdom is one characteristic of God that his people can reflect. In fact, he wants us to be wise. The book of Proverbs speaks a lot about wisdom and folly, which we might think has to do with brain smarts. But in this context, wisdom and foolishness aren't as much connected to knowledge as they are moral character. The "fool" of Proverbs is someone whose moral character is lacking. The wise person is one who understands and appreciates the words of God and therefore reaps moral benefits.

Just like he did to King Solomon, who wrote many of the Proverbs, wisdom is given by God to those who ask for it. God never wants us to stop seeking his good gifts in our lives. These virtues bring us closer to him and help us better share his light with the world.

DAY 42

"I have more insight than all my teachers, for I meditate on your statutes."

—PSALM 119:99

Sometimes it's hard to sift out the meanings of Bible words. All languages have limitations, and unless we study ancient Hebrew, Greek, and a little Aramaic, we're reading the words of Scripture in an English translation. So it's important to be sure we don't apply English-only meanings to the words of the Bible when the original languages don't carry the same meanings.

Which might lead us to wonder . . . Does wisdom mean the same thing as intelligence? In English, wisdom is sometimes described as the application of knowledge. So, do you first have to be intelligent or book smart to be able to have the kind of wisdom described in the Bible?

Book smarts or a high IQ are useful gifts from God, but they're not the same as the spiritual gift of wisdom. Whether you're blessed with a sharp mind or you feel like you're struggling to keep up in class, wisdom is for you. God is willing to grant us understanding when we ask—no SAT scores required.

DAY 43

"Tell all the skilled workers to whom I have given wisdom in such matters that they are to make garments for Aaron, for his consecration, so he may serve me as priest."

—EXODUS 28:3

Have you ever struggled in school? Is there a particular subject that makes you feel like you'll never get it? Sometimes that feeling spills into our Christian life too, especially when it comes to reading the Bible. Bible study can be overwhelming if you don't feel like you're gifted with book smarts. Maybe you feel like it's too complex, too complicated, and you'll never make sense of it.

And maybe you feel like you got skipped over on the day God was giving out the gifts that matter to him. But, wait! This verse from Exodus proves that sad notion wrong. It says God had given wisdom in *craftsmanship* to certain people so they might make the tabernacle the way he wanted it. It's not assuming too much to suppose he's given wisdom in the arts, sports, building, cleaning, growing, entertaining, and a whole host of other areas too. Everyone was made to shine in some way, and we're called to use the gifts we're born with—and even those we're not—to the best of our abilities. What's one area you're gifted? How can you shine in that area to give glory to God?

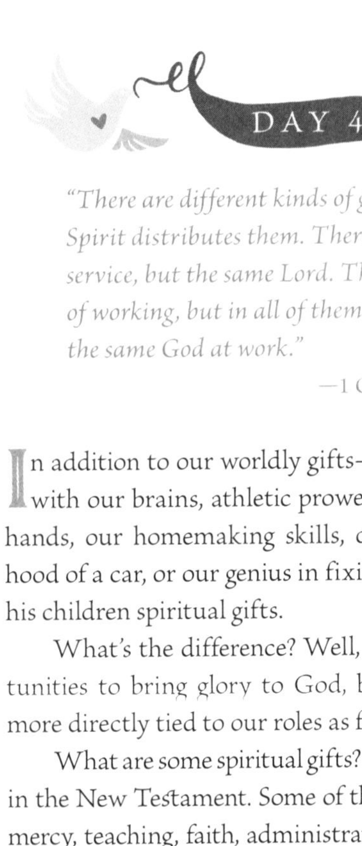

DAY 44

"There are different kinds of gifts, but the same Spirit distributes them. There are different kinds of service, but the same Lord. There are different kinds of working, but in all of them and in everyone it is the same God at work."

—1 CORINTHIANS 12:4–6

In addition to our worldly gifts—the ones that have to do with our brains, athletic prowess, artistic abilities, crafty hands, our homemaking skills, our knowledge under the hood of a car, or our genius in fixing computers—God gives his children spiritual gifts.

What's the difference? Well, all of our gifts are opportunities to bring glory to God, but our spiritual gifts are more directly tied to our roles as followers of Jesus.

What are some spiritual gifts? There are quite a few listed in the New Testament. Some of them are: giving, leadership, mercy, teaching, faith, administration, healing, discernment, hospitality, and wisdom. All of these are very good gifts from God. Do you know what your spiritual gifts are? If not, a good way to find out is to start serving in your church. See what type of ministry opportunities really click well with you, and serve your heart out. God wants us to use our gifts!

DAY 45

"If any of you lacks wisdom, you should ask God, who gives generously to all without finding fault, and it will be given to you."

—JAMES 1:5

What if you want more wisdom? Is this a limited-time-only sort of deal? God passed out wisdom to a chosen few when he was knitting them together in their mothers' wombs, and if you missed the boat, that's too bad?

No, of course not! James shows us that God always wants to give us more wisdom. When we seek good gifts for the sake of God's kingdom, God is faithful to respond to those prayers and give freely of his gifts. There's a bit of a Spider-Man situation happening there, of course. Remember that line? "With great power comes great responsibility." When you ask for spiritual gifts from God, be sure your heart is in the right place—those gifts are meant to bring glory to God, not ourselves. And also understand that when God gives us increased maturity in our spiritual gifts, we are required to use them even more carefully.

Side note—did you know the root of that Spider-Man quote is actually found in Luke 12:48? "From everyone who has been given much, much will be demanded; and from the one who has been entrusted with much, much more will be asked." Jesus is the original superhero.

DAY 46

"For God so loved the world that he gave his one and only Son, that whoever believes in him shall not perish but have eternal life."

—JOHN 3:16

God has made this truth so simple, it can be boiled down to one sentence, like this super-famous verse from the Gospel of John that perfectly explains salvation in such short order, it would fit in a tweet. On the other hand, scholars and theologians spend their entire lives searching the depths of this truth—all the things it implies, how it ties to other Scriptures, how it plays out in Christian living, how it was foreshadowed in the Old Testament, what it means for the second coming, and thousands of other angles—and still they don't reach the bottom of the pool.

The truth can be simple and complex, all at once. A verse from the Bible can have many layers of meaning. And that means God can speak into your life wherever you are. If you're happy, exhausted, hurt, celebrating, confused, or just feel like a baby in the faith, God still can and does speak to you. Right where you are. His truths will never change, but the way we understand them will forever be evolving, growing with us, and stretching to meet us where we are.

DAY 47

"I, even I, am he who blots out your transgressions, for my own sake, and remembers your sins no more."

—ISAIAH 43:25

If God's omniscience is true—if he knows all things actual and possible that have ever happened or will ever happen—can he really "forget" our sins? Does he secretly have a journal filled with every sin we've committed, and is he waiting to pounce on our failures?

That's a pretty horrible thought, isn't it? But there's good news. Verses like this one from Isaiah show us that, while God is most definitely omniscient, he "forgets" our sins in the sense that he doesn't consider them. Once we have accepted Jesus as our savior, our sins are no longer held against us. While God knows our mistakes as facts, they have no bearing on our relationship with him. There's no grudge. They've been covered by the blood of Jesus, and therefore are no longer held to our account.

So is there a "sin ledger" somewhere with your name on it? Perhaps. But every single line in that ledger would be crossed out with "Jesus paid" written in the margin. That's the promise God gives to his children.

DAY 48

"Do not be like them, for your Father knows what you need before you ask him."

—MATTHEW 6:8

The thought of an all-knowing God could sound a little intimidating at first. I mean . . . God knows *everything* about each of us? That means everything we do and say—the good, the bad, the ugly. And all the unspoken thoughts we filter before they leave our mouths—yep, God knows those too. Yikes.

But instead of making us fearful, this truth can bring us comfort. God's adored daughter can rest in his perfect wisdom and complete knowledge. The Bible even says God knows about our needs before we've asked him. And that's because God doesn't just know. He cares.

What's one thing you've been afraid to ask God for? What's a secret longing buried deep in your heart that you've hesitated to give a voice? Ask him. He already knows.

DAY 49

"And even the very hairs of your head are all numbered."

—MATTHEW 10:30

Scientists estimate there are about thirty-seven trillion cells in a human body. We might as well say "a bazillion kajillion." Neither really sounds like a real number. Have you ever seen thirty-seven trillion anything? That's about 5,193 times as many people as there on the entire planet. Maybe one day one of us will get to see $37,000,000,000,000. But the chances are probably pretty slim!

Thirty-seven trillion cells in your body, and yet every single one of them is known by God. He knows every fiber of your being. Every cell, every hair. Every thought, every feeling, every hope, every dream.

You are known and loved, not by a God who made the world, spun it into motion, then promptly walked away. No, God is still intimately involved with the tiniest details of his beloved creatures. And that includes you!

"But God chose the foolish things of the world to shame the wise; God chose the weak things of the world to shame the strong."

—1 CORINTHIANS 1:27

The way the world works makes sense to our human minds. Athletes, actors, singers, and others with talent receive honor, fame, and money. The world's system is merit-based. And when someone is famous for nothing, the world finds it very annoying. Our culture loves to hate the "famous for being famous" folks because they throw off our merit-based system.

But God doesn't work this way at all. The world values the best in everything—business, arts, athletics, academics—but God values the faithful. We should still strive for excellence. When God's children excel in their talents or succeed in their chosen fields, these accomplishments bring honor to God. But God doesn't select his servants because they're "the best." In fact, God often chooses roles for us that are far outside anything that makes sense.

The shy girl who is a gifted evangelist. The girl who is afraid to fly being called as a missionary. The former agnostic girl writing devotionals to strengthen the faith of others. What's the most unlikely task God would call you to? Pray about it. Maybe that's the exact place he'd like to use you.

DAY 51

"When pride comes, then comes disgrace, but with humility comes wisdom."

—PROVERBS 11:2

God really does like to flip the world's system on its head. When you get the things valued by the world—money, fame, success—it's hard to guard your heart against pride. And in God's view, disgrace follows pride.

By contrast, the humble servant of God is rewarded with wisdom. Remember our definition of wisdom? Choosing the best goals by the best means possible. We know God does this perfectly, but the Bible tells us that our humility is rewarded with wisdom too.

See how these things tie together? Someone wrapped up in pride, seeking her own glory, isn't likely to choose the best plan for her life or the best means to get there—at least not according to God's standards! When we seek God's ways in humility, he will lead us down the best paths for our lives.

"The fear of the L*ORD is the beginning of knowledge, but fools despise wisdom and instruction."*

—PROVERBS 1:7

Some of us are crazy enough to love to study. Like Hermione Granger, we're happiest buried beneath texts and maps and reference books. Maybe even a few scrolls. Don't hate on the scrolls! And *of course* it's not a waste of time to study dead languages or the cultural factors that influenced the writings of Ancient Mesopotamia . . . especially when you can use your Latin to ace your SAT reading section.

Studying will teach you facts. It can help you form opinions. But what does God say about *true* knowledge, the knowledge that matters? Once again, we have to adjust our thinking to try to get God's perspective because it's quite different from the world's. Proverbs says *the fear of the Lord* is the beginning of knowledge. What? Not the study of dead languages?!

How is fear of—or respect for—God the beginning of knowledge? Respecting God allows us to understand his rules and grasp his great love for us. When we start to view our studies, our lives, Scripture, and the world through this God-lens, we can gain true knowledge and wisdom.

DAY 53

"For all have sinned and fall short of the glory of God."

—ROMANS 3:23

When we fail, sometimes it feels like the world is closing in, especially when we fail to achieve a goal that was really important to us. A class we wanted to ace. A college we wanted to get into. A friendship we wanted to cultivate. A part we wanted in a play, or a championship game we really wanted to win.

Even more stinging is moral failure. When we know we didn't measure up to the Bible's standard—to God's standard—that really hurts. Not to mention the fact that moral failure often brings with it worldly consequences, and those are *never* fun.

But God is never surprised by our failings. He's not shocked when we don't reach our worldly goals, and he's not shocked when we fall short in our faith. He always wants us to do better, but he's not surprised when we show our imperfections. He knows our faults, failings, and setbacks before we do, and he still calls us adored.

DAY 54

"Record my misery; list my tears on your scroll—are they not in your record?"

—PSALM 56:8

How many tears do you suppose each thirty-seven-trillion-cell human body produces in a lifetime? One for every cell we have? Maybe. Even if it's not quite that many, it's safe to say the tears of each lifetime will be significant. More if you love watching chick flicks.

Did you know God knows every single one of those tears? Every tear, every sorrow, every silent wail when you can't even muster actual tears, and every ugly cry when you can't make the tears stop—God knows them all. He holds those tears in the palm of his universe-sized hand.

Take comfort in that, adored daughter. No pain goes unnoticed, unheard by God. His knowledge stretches to the darkest corners of your life and your heart. You are never alone or unloved in your hurt, sorrow, trauma, or suffering. God is listening.

DAY 55

"Where were you when I laid the earth's foundation? Tell me, if you understand. Who marked off its dimensions? Surely you know! Who stretched a measuring line across it?"

—JOB 38:4–5

If anyone knew about hardship, it was Job. The Bible specifically says the horrors he experienced had nothing to do with his sin. God was working on something bigger behind the scenes, but Job didn't know that. So Job spends a lot of chapters defending his honor against some judgmental friends and asking God *why*.

When God shows up to answer Job's questions, his response is . . . a little snarky. "Where were you when I created all these things, Job? That was you who helped me build the earth, right? Cool! Please keep telling me how to run it, won't you?" God continues on for two chapters. And then Job responds and says, "Whoa. My bad. I misspoke, but I get it now." (Paraphrasing.)

The point is, while God is there in our sorrow, we don't always get to know the "whys" of our suffering. Sometimes, despite our prayers, weeping, claims of innocence, and cries for mercy, we simply have to humble ourselves and accept that God is God. *He* is the one with perfect wisdom and the ultimate plan, and he is working his wise plan even when we don't know the "whys."

DAY 56

"These are the things God has revealed to us by his Spirit. The Spirit searches all things, even the deep things of God. For who knows a person's thoughts except their own spirit within them? In the same way no one knows the thoughts of God except the Spirit of God."

—1 CORINTHIANS 2:10–11

Is it possible to know God? We've taken a hard look at two of God's many traits—his unchangeableness and his wisdom—and God seems impossibly big. Huge. Too huge for our tiny human minds and hearts.

And in some ways, that's true. This verse from First Corinthians shows us that the only one who knows God fully is the Holy Spirit. And, really, the rest of us would probably explode if God tried to make his full mind known to us. Remember how he hid Moses in the rock and only showed a small portion of his glory so Moses wouldn't be burned up? Yeah, we would need an entire mountain of rock.

But in his wisdom, bringing about his good plan, God reveals himself to us in Scripture. He speaks to our hearts through the Holy Spirit. And he shows himself most plainly in the man Jesus. In Jesus, we see God in ways that are perhaps easier for us to wrap our human minds around. In Jesus, we see God in action, and we gain our ultimate example.

"This mystery is that through the gospel the Gentiles are heirs together with Israel, members together of one body, and sharers together in the promise in Christ Jesus."

—EPHESIANS 3:6

God's good plan includes—and has always included—diversity. This is a big deal in our modern world. And it was just as big a deal back in the days when Paul wrote these words.

We can feel the undercurrents of ethnic tension in the New Testament. There's a complex history behind the Hebrew disdain for the Samaritans, and the Jews themselves have been an oppressed people throughout much of history. When we consider these facts, and when we look around at our modern struggle to stamp out racism and discrimination, how much more amazing is it that God has always had diversity as part of his plan?

God values every people group, every nation, every color on earth. Consider what you can do today to help show the love of God to those who are different than you.

"For I desire mercy, not sacrifice, and acknowledgment of God rather than burnt offerings."

—HOSEA 6:6

Wow, what a great message of grace from the New Testament. Wait a second . . . Hosea is one of the Old Testament prophets! Can it be that the law-centered Old Testament shows us glimmers of God's ultimate plan of salvation through grace?

More than glimmers, actually. From this verse, and others like it, we see that God's plan, while revealed more and more fully over time, has always been the same. He has always looked at the heart of a person, rather than the outward actions. He has always valued faith over simply following the "letter of the law."

From Abraham to Ruth to Hosea, we see that God's plan for the redemption of mankind has faith at its heart. It's important—of greatest importance—that we don't simply go through the motions of loving God. Outward actions matter. Prayer, going to church, doing good works, showing others the love of Jesus, and reading our Bibles are all excellent things God wants us to do. But is there faith in your heart? Faith must be at the root of all the good things we do for God.

DAY 59

"'The days are coming,' declares the Lord, 'when I will make a new covenant with the people of Israel and with the people of Judah.'"

—JEREMIAH 31:31

Like faith, the savior has always been at the heart of God's plan. The prophet Jeremiah spoke these words, foretelling the new covenant that would be ushered in by Jesus, hundreds of years before Mary went into labor in a stable in Bethlehem. God's plan doesn't change—it just comes into greater focus as he reveals himself more fully.

So why should that matter to us? Obviously, these truths matter for our spiritual lives. But they also make a difference in our daily lives. When we study the way God has worked throughout history, we get a better sense of who he is and how he relates to us. If God has had a big, master plan since the beginning of time—one that has been centered around faith in Jesus—do you think he has a good plan for your life? Can you trust him with your future? Yes! God has a good plan for you that will be brought about in his time. Trust in it.

DAY 60

"And the peace of God, which transcends all understanding, will guard your hearts and your minds in Christ Jesus."

—PHILIPPIANS 4:7

What's the best take-away we can have from knowing we serve a perfectly wise, all-knowing God? Peace that "transcends all understanding," as Philippians says. The result of trusting in God's plan and leaning on his knowledge instead of our own leads us to peace that is beyond anything that can be explained or makes any kind of sense. That's peace that "transcends understanding."

Like many spiritual truths, it's simple. But it's not necessarily easy. Our human wills want us to go our own ways, follow our own hearts. Waiting on God when we don't know what's on the horizon and we don't get the whys of what we're dealing with is really, really difficult. It takes practice.

But when we get there—when we're able to trust the God we serve—we can walk through life in peace. Do you feel anxious or worried about anything today? Remember, God's got you.

DAY 61

"That conforms to the gospel concerning the glory of the blessed God, which he entrusted to me."

—1 TIMOTHY 1:11

We hear the word "blessed" a lot these days. It has become a popular hashtag on social media, even. But do we really understand what it means? And what does it mean when we say God is "blessed" or we talk about his "blessedness"?

The Greek word Paul uses here that is translated as "blessed" (*makarios*) means happiness. Delight. Joy. And God's happiness is delight in its richest, deepest sense—the happiness that comes from delighting fully in himself. God's blessedness means that he also delights fully in anything that reflects his character. Any trait, characteristic, deed, thought, person, or object of creation that reflects God's character is delightful to him.

You have a God who is delighted in you. He's happy, joyful, and blessed when you reflect him. Think of the way a mom is delighted by her small child who is growing to be independent and thoughtful. Think of the way that mom smiles at her little one. That's how God smiles at us when we're doing and being the things that please him.

DAY 62

"As a young man marries a young woman, so will your Builder marry you; as a bridegroom rejoices over his bride, so will your God rejoice over you."

—ISAIAH 62:5

Everyone feels rejected sometimes. And some of us feel rejected a lot. Feeling unpopular, unwanted, or unloved is pretty terrible. But God doesn't see us that way, ever. In you, God sees a reflection of himself, and that's delightful to him. In fact, Isaiah compares the way God feels about his people to the way a groom feels about his bride.

You've seen newlyweds before. They're always starry-eyed, obnoxiously happy, and convinced their other half is the greatest human on the face of the planet. That's the level at which God loves us. Like a groom loves his bride. *You* are loved by God, and he delights in *you*.

We will all feel the sting of the world's rejection, but it's important we don't lose sight of God's perspective. It's the one that matters. And know that God doesn't reject you. So walk with the confidence of someone who is adored by her creator. Because you are.

DAY 63

"For who makes you different from anyone else? What do you have that you did not receive?"

—1 CORINTHIANS 4:7A

Have you ever looked at someone else and thought, "If only I were like her . . . "? Whether it's related to our looks, our intelligence, our talents, our gifts, or our circumstances, it's hard not to compare ourselves to others sometimes . . . and find that we come up short.

But God created a very specific you. He could have given you any personality, any set of gifts, any face, any body type, but he chose the one you have. Sometimes that might make us feel like filing a complaint. "Excuse me, God? I think you made a mistake on the day you were handing out athletic ability (or perfect skin, excellent grades, a drama-free family). Can I have a redo?" Ever been there?

When we learn to accept our own unique set of traits and characteristics, imperfect though they may be, we reflect the person God created us to be. Embrace the specific *you* God made and delight in your uniqueness. God certainly does.

"For we are God's handiwork, created in Christ Jesus to do good works, which God prepared in advance for us to do."
—EPHESIANS 2:10

Do you ever wonder why God created you the way he did? Maybe you're an outgoing people-person who loves meeting new friends and organizing big groups. Or maybe you're reserved—a thinker and observer. Maybe you like to ponder deep, complicated issues, or maybe you prefer to keep your focus on the practical, everyday matters of life.

Each of these unique personality types—and thousands of others—is specially equipped to do certain kinds of work. And our all-knowing God planned it that way on purpose. You were created with a set of traits geared toward a certain type of service. That outgoing people-person would be great at organizing a church outreach event. The reserved thinker would be the perfect person to plan a small-group bible study. Maybe the deep, complicated issue-tackler is called to be a pastor or counselor or teacher. Someone great at practical issues makes an excellent church administrator.

However you're built, there are ways to serve perfectly suited to you. And sometimes, God surprises us by calling us to areas outside our comfort zones to stretch us and glorify himself through our weaknesses. So roll up your sleeves and get to it!

DAY 65

"For from him and through him and for him are all things. To him be the glory forever! Amen."

—ROMANS 11:36

In the days of cyber-bullying and the body-image issues so many young women deal with, it's really important to reinforce the message that you are loved and you are good enough, just as you are. No upgrades required. But is it possible to have too much self-esteem? In our effort to combat the negative messages of the world, can we go too far?

Absolutely. In fact, the Bible has a whole lot to say about this destructive kind of pride. When we've crossed over from embracing ourselves and our secure position in God's love to exalting ourselves, we've gone too far. Remember, God delights in us because we reflect *him*. All good things come from him, and he should be the recipient of the glory.

So we must balance accepting and appreciating ourselves with walking in humility. Never be afraid to say "I was wrong," or "I'm sorry," or "I don't know." Being handcrafted and adored by God doesn't mean we're perfect.

"The heavens declare the glory of God; the skies proclaim the work of his hands."

—PSALM 19:1

God delights in his creation. Nature reflects God's beauty, and we should delight in it too.

In our modern world, it'd be pretty easy to go from building to car to building to car and never stop to experience nature. Maybe you're surrounded by the concrete of the suburbs or the high-rise buildings of a major metropolis. Or maybe you live on a farm, surrounded by nature all the time, and you're chuckling at the rest of us right now.

No matter where you live, you can enjoy God's handiwork. Make an effort to get outside and experience the things God has created. Check out parks or walking trails in your area. Go for an easy hike if you're a beginner. Plan a camping weekend and appreciate the peace and stillness of being away from the bustle of regular life. Or even just get out into your backyard or your patio and grow something. Urban gardens are awesome. It's amazing what you can produce in a planter box.

DAY 67

"God saw all that he had made, and it was very good. And there was evening, and there was morning—the sixth day."

—GENESIS 1:31

The things God has created are good. He is glorified by them. But he made man the highest of the created beings and gave us "dominion" over everything else. We're the dominant creatures on earth, and that's just as God designed it to be.

But what does dominion look like? It's important we don't run roughshod over the earth and the creatures that live in it. God wants us to be good stewards of what he's entrusted to us, and that applies to his beautiful creation.

Consider how your actions might affect the things God has created. The environment is important, as are the animals that depend on it, but God's creation also includes mankind. Balance care for the earth and its creatures with care for your fellow humans. Practical ways to get involved are endless. Try volunteering with a ministry or nonprofit that feeds the hungry, picks up litter, clothes and houses the homeless, rescues abandoned animals, or focuses on wildlife conservation.

DAY 68

"Therefore, since we have these promises, dear friends, let us purify ourselves from everything that contaminates body and spirit, perfecting holiness out of reverence for God."

—2 CORINTHIANS 7:1

God is blessed by everything that reflects his character, and that includes us. There are many ways we can reflect God's character, but one of the biggest is by striving for holiness.

It may feel impossible to refuse sin when we're surrounded by it. And we are, constantly. Our culture has lost almost all appearance of righteousness and instead seems to be focused on pride, greed, and a me-first mentality. So how do we strive for holiness when we're pushed on all sides by ungodly pressure?

The first question we should ask ourselves about anything we wish to pursue is, "What would God say about it?" Have you ever seen those WWJD bracelets from the 1990s? "What Would Jesus Do" has become a cliché, but it's a solid principle to follow if we wish to pursue holiness in our lives—and we should! What would Jesus do in this situation? Or, what would Jesus say about this? Or, how would Jesus respond to this person or that opportunity or this pursuit? When we keep that question at the forefront of our minds—then respond accordingly—we can, inch by inch, pursue holiness in our lives.

DAY 69

"Whoever claims to love God yet hates a brother or sister is a liar. For whoever does not love their brother and sister, whom they have seen, cannot love God, whom they have not seen."

—1 JOHN 4:20

What should be the defining characteristic of a Christian? The number of times she's read the Bible cover-to-cover? Awesome goal, but no. Her perfect church attendance? Important ideal, but also no. Her activism for a certain political party? It's fine to enjoy politics, and voting is important, but still no.

John says that if a Christian claims to love God but hates a brother or sister, they don't really know or love God. Wow! The single defining characteristic of a Christian is how much we love others. How do we treat those who are different—who don't share our history, culture, language, or skin color? How do we treat those who have less than us, whether in material wealth, the pursuit of holiness, or some other way?

If we don't show every single person God-sized love, we're missing the point of our time on earth as Christians. Sometimes love looks like listening. Sometimes it looks like being there. Sometimes love is communing with the broken-hearted, lighting the path out of darkness. How can you love like Jesus today? Whose path can you light?

DAY 70

"For if you forgive other people when they sin against you, your heavenly Father will also forgive you."
—MATTHEW 6:14

Friends are awesome. Even those of us who have only a few very close friends, rather than a huge crew, love and value our friends deeply. Shared experiences, laughter, and heartache make friendships some of the most important relationships in our lives.

But what happens when a friend hurts you? What about when a friend who you thought was a close confidant in your inner circle betrays you or becomes jealous and tries to tear you down? Conflict happens sometimes, even between the best of friends. Gentle, direct communication can be a relationship-saver. But when someone turns truly toxic, it's okay to distance yourself. Boundaries are important, and when attempts at resolution fail, cutting ties is appropriate, even when it hurts and we mourn the relationship we lost.

But forgiveness is a vital—if difficult—part of the equation. Seeking retaliation, gossiping, or carrying bitterness about a former-friend not only hurts them, it hurts you too. Even if you're one hundred percent in the right and the former-friend *never* apologizes, forgive them anyway. That's the way God forgives us. God-sized forgiveness brings peace to your heart and helps you and your former-friend avoid unnecessary drama.

DAY 71

"Be on your guard; stand firm in the faith; be courageous; be strong."

—1 CORINTHIANS 16:13

The Bible is clear that God puts authority figures in our lives. Our parents, for starters, and later, teachers, bosses, and even the government. Submitting to authority is an act of humility and is often wise, especially when those authority figures are loving parents who want the best for our lives.

But what happens when someone in authority over us is . . . wrong? Gasp! Wait, you're not shocked that your parents are wrong sometimes? Maybe even more obvious is that our government can be quite wrong. Perhaps you've studied governments around the world that are openly hostile to Christians and the persecution believers in those countries experience. Don't forget to pray for those brothers and sisters!

While respecting authority is an important and godly thing to do, standing firm in our convictions is equally important when authority figures step on the toes of our faith or God's word. You can disagree or oppose peacefully and with a respectful attitude. Stand firm in your convictions when you have God's word on your side.

"A perverse person stirs up conflict, and a gossip separates close friends."

—PROVERBS 16:28

There's a lot of talk in the Bible about guarding our mouths from hateful speech, gossip, and words that seek to tear down God and others. But if the Bible had been written today, there might be even more verses about this same principle, except with regard to our keyboards.

As easy as it is to speak hurtful words with our tongues, it's even easier to do the same thing online. Why is that? Technology creates a sense of safety in anonymity. The Internet feels anonymous, so we can mistakenly get the idea that there's little accountability for our words online. People feel free to say horrible things to each other—things they d never say to anyone's face—because the Internet seems like a faceless mob.

But there are real people behind each of those screen names. Are we treating them like real people? Are we avoiding needless battles by steering clear of gossip and trolling? Let's work to keep our mouths—and fingertips—innocent of unnecessary conflict.

DAY 73

"All Scripture is God-breathed and is useful for teaching, rebuking, correcting and training in righteousness, so that the servant of God may be thoroughly equipped for every good work."

—2 TIMOTHY 3:16–17

God took special care when creating his Word. It was a centuries-long process, and he used many willing servant-authors to tell his story. Since then, the Bible has been carefully preserved, translated, examined, and then translated many more times, as older original-language documents are unearthed from the far corners of the world. What an amazing process!

God delights in his word, and we can too. Continuing to read, study, and learn from God's word is one of the greatest things we can do to nourish our faith. It helps us understand God, Jesus, God's plan for salvation, and his historical relationship with his people.

Studying the Scriptures also keeps us from being pew-warmers. When we're constantly filling our minds with God's commands and promises, it becomes almost impossible to be an Easter-Christmas church-goer or Sunday-morning Christian. God wants more from us than to simply sit in a pew on certain holidays or days of the week. He wants us to actively live out our faith. And we can turn to the Scriptures to discover just what that looks like.

DAY 74

"Flee from sexual immorality. All other sins a person commits are outside the body, but whoever sins sexually, sins against their own body."

—1 CORINTHIANS 6:18

Let's face it: sex is an awkward topic for a lot of people. Many parents, pastors, teachers, and mentors cringe at the idea of discussing sex, and frankly, many of those they parent, pastor, teach, or mentor wouldn't be too interested in the conversation, either. It's highly personal, and that can make it difficult to discuss.

But it's an important discussion. Sexual purity—avoiding sexual immorality as defined by the Bible—is something spoken of in both the Old and New Testaments. And in our modern culture, sexual purity is increasingly difficult to maintain.

It's important we don't give in to the world's message—that sex is no big deal. But it's also important we don't swing too far the other direction and make sex taboo, only spoken of in hushed tones, if at all. Uncomfortable as the conversations may be, it's important for God's sons and daughters to understand that sex isn't inherently sinful or unholy. It's one of God's many good gifts, created to be shared in the context of marriage. So, while God has placed boundaries on sex, and we're commanded to stay within those boundaries, don't be afraid to start discussions or ask questions about this subject.

DAY 75

"Whatever your hand finds to do, do it with all your might, for in the realm of the dead, where you are going, there is neither working nor planning nor knowledge nor wisdom."

—ECCLESIASTES 9:10

Have you ever had to do something you felt completely unequipped to do? Running a mile in a certain time, taking a really difficult final exam, writing a particular college admissions essay, working a job where you felt out of your depth, or maybe completing a task at church you were dreading.

God is perfectly excellent in all he does, and he's perfectly blessed. Since we're not God, we'll never achieve quite that level of bliss until we reach eternity. But we can reflect God's blessedness by striving for excellence in all that we do, even those tasks where we feel overwhelmed.

What does that look like, practically speaking? Well, it may sound cliché, but striving for excellence is simply doing your best. It's hanging in there and not giving up because it's hard. It's working to get better, whether you're naturally gifted at the task or not. It's imagining you have Jesus beside you—not grading you, but cheering you on and encouraging you to work hard and work well. So whatever the day brings you—tasks you're excited about or tasks you're dreading—do your best!

DAY 76

"He will love you and bless you and increase your numbers. He will bless the fruit of your womb, the crops of your land—your grain, new wine and olive oil—the calves of your herds and the lambs of your flocks in the land he swore to your ancestors to give you. You will be blessed more than any other people; none of your men or women will be childless, nor will any of your livestock be without young."

—DEUTERONOMY 7:13–14

We've looked at God's blessedness—his delight in himself and all that reflects his character—but what does the Bible mean when it says *we* are blessed?

Blessings can be material, like those in this promise to the Israelites from Deuteronomy. Christians sometimes have mixed feelings about material blessings. It feels like a fine line between appreciation and materialistic greed to say we're "blessed" when we get a raise or are able to afford a new home or nice vacation.

But material things aren't, in themselves, bad. The Bible calls material things blessings, so it's okay to appreciate it if God provides your family with what you need to be comfortable. Many people around the world don't have these simple things, so appreciation is always appropriate. As long as the material blessings push you toward thankfulness and generosity toward others, it's okay to acknowledge your blessings!

DAY 77

"I will make them and the places surrounding my hill a blessing. I will send down showers in season; there will be showers of blessing. The trees will yield their fruit and the ground will yield its crops; the people will be secure in their land. They will know that I am the LORD, *when I break the bars of their yoke and rescue them from the hands of those who enslaved them."*

—EZEKIEL 34:26–27

Have you ever met a refugee? How about a war veteran? Have you ever been to a country where a battle has recently occurred? If you have talked to a refugee or combat veteran, or you've seen with your own eyes exactly what "war-torn" looks like, then you'll really be able to embrace this truth.

Sometimes, God's blessing looks like security and peace. This is true on a national level (though we should be very careful about rushing to judgment against nations dealing with conflict or disaster), but it's also true on a personal level. And here's a secret: faith allows you to find personal peace and security, even when the world around you is in an uproar of conflict or chaos.

How can you grab some peace today? Whether it's an extra moment to sit in quiet prayer and reflection, or an exuberant celebration of all the good God has brought into your life, snag it! The ability to be at peace or rest securely in God's love is one of his greatest blessings.

DAY 78

"Yet he has not left himself without testimony: He has shown kindness by giving you rain from heaven and crops in their seasons; he provides you with plenty of food and fills your hearts with joy."

—ACTS 14:17

Maybe your cup isn't exactly overflowing with wealth. Does that mean you're outside of God's favor? When jobs are lost, pay is cut, putting a meal on the table is a struggle, or you can't replace worn-out clothes, it can feel that way.

But sometimes, God's material blessing is provision instead of abundance. What's the difference? Provision is "just enough." Just enough to make it to tomorrow, to keep your belly full and your body clothed. Experiencing God's provision can make his presence even clearer than abundant blessing.

When we have more than enough of all we need, it's easy to believe we had some hand in getting it. *I* worked hard for that. *I* earned it. *I* made my own blessing. The focus becomes our own accomplishments and we can forget to give glory to God. But when we don't know where the next meal will come from, and it shows up anyway, God's hand is clear. We *know* it wouldn't have happened without him, and so he gets the glory, no question.

So whether you're experiencing abundance or provision, you are blessed.

DAY 79

"Praise be to the God and Father of our Lord Jesus Christ, who has blessed us in the heavenly realms with every spiritual blessing in Christ."

—EPHESIANS 1:3

Many blessings aren't material at all. In fact, some of our greatest blessings are spiritual. That's why, no matter what circumstances we're experiencing, we can always call ourselves a blessed people. In the midst of national turmoil, personal tragedy, or hard times, every single Christian on earth is blessed.

What do spiritual blessings look like? Supernatural patience, endurance, forgiveness, peace, and love are all spiritual blessings. How do you know if it's supernatural? When it's peace that makes no sense in your situation. When you have patience when any reasonable person would've exploded. When you endure hardship that can't even be imagined. When you've been hurt so deeply, it should leave scars for the rest of your life, and instead, you're able to forgive. When you have peace in the middle of a life-storm. When you love an enemy.

Those are all actions outside of man's standard operating procedure. Our first instinct may be to put ourselves first, to crush our enemies, to run away when things get difficult. But God's people are blessed to be able to practice a different standard operating procedure. The Holy Spirit helps us to walk like Jesus through these spiritual blessings.

DAY 80

"Everyone who calls on the name of the Lord will be saved."

—ROMANS 10:13

Maybe you feel like you were skipped over on "spiritual blessing day" because you're never patient or peaceful and you find forgiveness, endurance, or loving others a struggle. Don't worry. You weren't passed over. Like all of us, you're a work in progress, and God's got you. If you recognize your struggles in these areas and you'd like to do better, you're doing it right!

No matter where we are on our personal growth journey, there's one blessing we can all claim in its fullest sense: salvation. This verse from Romans is so cool. Every. Single. Person. who calls on the name of the Lord will be saved. No exceptions. If anyone realizes she falls short of God's standard and she wants Jesus to be her savior, he is. It's as simple as that.

So, on those days where you feel especially unspiritual, remember this—you are saved! Jesus redeemed you! You're blessed and adored, and that's worth celebrating.

DAY 81

"Awake, LORD! Why do you sleep? Rouse yourself! Do not reject us forever. Why do you hide your face and forget our misery and oppression?"

—PSALM 44:23–24

God's blessedness speaks to his delight—his happiness—and we want to reflect that. But what about when happiness eludes us? What about when it feels like all the joy has been sucked from our lives and we've been cast down into a pit? Most people experience this at some point, and it ranges from having "down" days sometimes to dealing with real depression.

Whatever the source of your sadness, know that God is with you. Sadness is not a sin. The psalms show us this, especially King David's writings. He cried out to God, asked why, wept over his persecution and his own sin. David was brokenhearted a lot. And David, despite his flaws, was called a man after God's own heart.

We can cry out. We can ask God why. We can weep and mourn. But we never have to feel alone. God is always close to the brokenhearted.

DAY 82

"The Lord is good, a refuge in times of trouble. He cares for those who trust in him."

—NAHUM 1:7

The word *refuge* can bring to mind some cool pictures. A lighthouse in a stormy sea. A warm cabin in a blizzard. Maybe even a dwelling burrowed into the side of a hill, like a hobbit hole. A refuge is a safe, secure place, especially when everything outside isn't so safe, whether from a roiling sea, a deluge of snow, or . . . orcs.

God is our ultimate refuge. When we're experiencing low points, whether they're short-lived or a longer-term trial, we can take refuge in God's goodness. He is our safe space, like a lighthouse protecting us from battering waves or a cozy cabin sheltering us from swirling snow. Or, yes, even a snug hobbit hole guarding us from orcs on the hunt. Sometimes our troubles feel the most like those bloodthirsty orcs.

But when we trust in God, he promises to see us through the dark times—to care for us and make sure we know we're not forgotten. Hide in him as your refuge. Let God be your ultimate safe place.

DAY 83

"But ask the animals, and they will teach you, or the birds in the sky, and they will tell you; or speak to the earth, and it will teach you, or let the fish in the sea inform you. Which of all these does not know that the hand of the LORD has done this? In his hand is the life of every creature and the breath of all mankind."

—JOB 12:7–10

Science now confirms what God's people have known for a long time. Creation is good. Being out in nature has been proven to help fight down moods. If you're looking for a very practical way to respond when happiness eludes you, go outside!

Fresh air, vitamin D from the sun, and taking a few moments out of your typical routine to enjoy natural beauty are all powerful weapons to ward off depressive moods. But you know what's even more helpful? Using that time outside to reflect on God. Put aside the problems bringing you down at the moment, and focus on the wonder of the nature surrounding you. A single leaf shows us the intricacy of the world God has created, and shifting our focus to God's awesomeness can help vault us from that dark pit—or at least help us remember that even when we're in the pit, we serve a big, capable God. He'll see you through this.

DAY 84

"I call out to the Lord, and he answers me from his holy mountain."

—PSALM 3:4

Sadness and isolation are like a vicious cycle. We feel sad, and it leads us to isolating ourselves. Then we're even sadder because we're isolated, which leads us to withdraw even more. Or maybe the cycle started with isolation and that led to our sadness.

But no matter how cut off, lonely, or down we feel, we're never truly alone. God is always with us, and he wants us to talk to him. Prayer is one of our greatest privileges as God's people.

The words don't have to be spoken aloud, but if you feel like it, by all means, speak to him aloud. Whether the words are audible to anyone else or not, God hears them. When we spill our hearts to God in prayer, it helps us better understand the truth that we're not alone. We can "know" God is always there, but do we actually believe that, heart and soul? Start pouring out your thoughts and feelings to God on a regular basis, and the truth will sink deeper and deeper into you.

DAY 85

"Do not be afraid, for I am with you; I will bring your children from the east and gather you from the west."

—ISAIAH 43:5

The pit can be a scary place. Going through a season of sadness can feel like a dark veil has been thrown over your face. You can still see everything, for the most part, but a dark haze has blurred the edges—made things you were sure of suddenly feel less real, less distinct.

And that feeling is frightening. But God tells us we never have to be afraid because he's with us. Those things we knew to be real and true are still real and true. It's our vision that has changed, not reality or the truth. Push aside your fear with your faith. We pray for God's help in casting off our veils so we can once again see with clarity.

Think back to a time in your life that was really scary. Can you see now, given some perspective, how God was with you the whole time? He's with you now, too, and he'll be with you during all your future difficulties. Don't be afraid!

DAY 86

"Surely you have granted him unending blessings and made him glad with the joy of your presence."

—PSALM 21:6

Unending blessings. Eternal blessings. One long string of blessings. Blessings and joy and happiness forever. That's what we have on the horizon. Talk about something to look forward to.

Sometimes, when life is at its hardest, a shift in thinking can help see us through the dark time. This life on earth is not the end of our existence. In fact, compared to eternity, one hundred years in this life is just a short sneeze on our timelines. And eternity is going to be pretty amazing. God has promised us a new earth. Creation the way it was meant to be, without the effects of sin to mar it. Or us.

And when we're eternity-minded, we realize pain and hardship are temporary. That truth can be enough to help move *out* of our dark time in this life and embrace the joy and peace God offers to us in spite of difficult circumstances.

DAY 87

"As the deer pants for streams of water, so my soul pants for you, my God."

—PSALM 42:1

All our souls are thirsty. The ultimate thirst-quencher is God, of course, but he gives us other good things to satisfy our parched souls. Surrounding ourselves with those soul-quenching good things can remind us how excellent God is and how blessed we are.

Soul-quenchers are found in our relationships. Maybe for you, that's a beloved sibling, a best friend, or a close parent. Soul-quenchers can be found in our hobbies. Maybe that's a sport you play, the mountain of books you'd like to read, or the art you love to create. Soul-quenchers can even be found in the smallest of things. A delicious hot drink on a cold day, a favorite treat, a warm summer rain, or snuggling a beloved pet.

Make a list of the things that satisfy your soul. When it's difficult to find your happiness, return to this list. Indulge in your soul-quenching activities, people, and small loves. Let them remind you of God's goodness.

"Let those who love the LORD hate evil, for he guards the lives of his faithful ones and delivers them from the hand of the wicked."

—PSALM 97:10

In general, we know God delights in us when we reflect his character. But how can we specifically reflect God's blessedness? We can take pleasure in the things that please him.

That means our happiness and joy should come from things God would call "good." Small blessings, large blessings, spiritual blessings, God's creation, fellow believers, serving others—all these things are good, and when we take pleasure in them, we mirror the pleasure God takes in them.

On the flipside, we shouldn't take pleasure in the things God dislikes. Actually hates. The Bible uses the word "hate" to describe how God feels about certain things. Proverbs lists some: haughty eyes (disdainful arrogance), a lying tongue, hands that shed innocent blood, a wicked heart, feet quick to rush into evil, and those who stir up conflict. When we turn away from such things, we turn toward things God finds pleasing—those things from which we should be finding our happiness.

DAY 89

"Take delight in the LORD, and he will give you the desires of your heart."

—PSALM 37:4

The ultimate source of our happiness is God, the one who isn't dependent on circumstances, ever. Friends rise and fall in importance in our lives and our parents won't always be with us when we go out into the world. Circumstances change. We go through great times and hard times. But through it all, God is there, always remaining the same. And if he is the ultimate source of our delight, we will always have his unending well of happiness to draw upon.

How do we get to know God better so that he becomes the source of our delight? God gives us his Spirit, but he has also revealed himself to us in a very concrete way—Scripture. We can know about his revealed character and his deeds by studying his word. And the clearest picture God has given us of himself is his son, Jesus. Because Jesus is a man, he makes God's character more understandable and relatable to us. We see God in the flesh through Jesus, and not only does that give us the ultimate example to follow, it can—and should—bring delight to our hearts.

DAY 90

"The LORD delights in those who fear him, who put their hope in his unfailing love."

—PSALM 147:11

Want to know something that should make us really happy? Our God is full of happiness, joy, and delight. Sometimes we read stories from the Bible about when God was exercising his wrath or God's judgment came down upon a particular person or group of people. That can be scary stuff to read. And God is absolutely a holy God who will not tolerate sin.

But God isn't some big ball of anger and hate. He's not a vengeful tyrant in the sky, looking to smite us at every turn, waiting for us to trip up, hoping we'll make a mistake so he can zap us with lightning. No, he's patient and kind, allowing countless opportunities for us to choose him, turn to him, and walk in his ways, gently embracing us when we've messed up and we return to him. He is the very embodiment of love, itself.

And this should cause us to rejoice in thankfulness. God loves us enough to steer us away from evil and toward himself, and what could give us more joy than that?

DAY 91

"The Lord bless you and keep you."

—NUMBERS 6:24

The word "blessed" has come under some fire recently because people use it so flippantly. It's one of the more popular hashtags on social media among Christians and non-Christians alike. So . . . is it a bad word to use? Should we shy away from saying we're blessed?

No matter how else anyone might misuse or misunderstand the word, you *are* blessed. It's not a humble-brag to say so. You are blessed with your unique temperament, your unique life. You are blessed with times of abundance and times of "just enough." You are blessed with gifts, talents, dreams, things to do, things to say. God is the source of all these good things, so it's okay to acknowledge them, as long as we also acknowledge God as our source. And as long as we understand that when times are lean, we feel like we're in the pit, or we're weathering a difficult storm, we're *still* blessed. Blessing in hardship is sometimes the deepest blessing of all.

So, walk like a blessed daughter of God today, because that's exactly what you are.

DAY 92

"Hang the curtain from the clasps and place the ark of the covenant law behind the curtain. The curtain will separate the Holy Place from the Most Holy Place."

—EXODUS 26:33

God's holiness is a really important concept woven throughout all Scripture. Both Old and New Testaments have a lot to say about it, and when that's the case, we should probably pay attention!

God's holiness means that he is separated from sin and fully devoted to seeking his own honor. God commanded the Israelites to set up the tabernacle in a way that reflected this separation. Not only was there a "Holy Place," but there was a separate "Most Holy Place," sometimes called the "Holy of Holies," and that's where God's presence dwelled among the Israelites. It's also where the high priest went once per year to offer atonement for the Israelite community's sins. One day per year, by one man—that's how frequently this part of the tabernacle was allowed to be used. Showing this separation from sin was important to God.

When Jesus took his last breath, the curtain that separated the Holy Place from the Most Holy Place in the temple ripped. Through Jesus's death, we now have access to God's presence in a way not even the Israelites did. And we're called to honor this close relationship with God by reflecting his holiness.

DAY 93

"For the LORD has chosen Jacob to be his own, Israel to be his treasured possession."

—PSALM 135:4

God has a long history of "setting apart." We see the principle in the tabernacle and temple having specific rooms for set purposes. We see it in the Levites being a tribe set apart for priestly service. And we see it in God's choosing of Isaac over Ishmael and Jacob over Esau.

But one of the clearest pictures of God setting apart something for himself is his choosing of the nation of Israel to be his people, selected out of all the many people groups on earth. God choosing and separating Israel should matter to us. Why? Aren't they just an ancient people group we read about in Bible history books?

No! God's choosing of Israel foreshadowed his choosing of Jesus's followers. He draws us, separates us from the world, calls us to holiness. We may not always understand why we've been called, but we can rest securely in the knowledge that we are. *We* are his new Israel, chosen to be his treasured, adored possession.

"Do not be yoked together with unbelievers. For what do righteousness and wickedness have in common? Or what fellowship can light have with darkness? What harmony is there between Christ and Belial? Or what does a believer have in common with an unbeliever? What agreement is there between the temple of God and idols? For we are the temple of the living God."

—2 CORINTHIANS 6:14–16

Do you have a close friend or family member who isn't a follower of Jesus yet? Most of us do. Or, even more difficult, do you know someone who is strongly opposed to Jesus? Who hates church, the Bible, and everything Christians stand for?

Few things make our hearts hurt worse. When we've discovered the love of Jesus, we want everyone in our lives to experience it too. When they don't, it's tough. Really tough. It doesn't make it any easier that the Bible has clear warnings against believers having close relationships with unbelievers.

So what does this mean? Do you have to walk away from all your non-Christian friends? No. If people who love Jesus shut themselves away from the world, how will others hear and see the Gospel? But we do need to be careful about opening the depths of our hearts to those who don't share our faith. If a relationship hinders our pursuit of holiness, it might be time to reconsider that friendship.

DAY 95

"You have stolen my heart, my sister, my bride; you have stolen my heart with one glance of your eyes, with one jewel of your necklace. How delightful is your love, my sister, my bride! How much more pleasing is your love than wine, and the fragrance of your perfume more than any spice!"

—SONG OF SONGS 4:9–10

Romance and holiness may not seem to go hand-in-hand. The idea of dating can become a big, scary wilderness where it feels like we're constantly dodging unholy landmines. So some people decide it's better to avoid it altogether. And that's a valid choice.

But romantic relationships are not inherently bad or dangerous. In fact there's actually romance *in* the Bible.

We can maintain holiness in our romantic relationships by choosing to wait until marriage for sex. If you're dating someone, make sure you agree on clear boundaries and concrete ways to avoid crossing those boundaries. And if your boyfriend is pressuring you to ignore your boundaries, reconsider that relationship. Anyone who makes you feel guilty about maintaining a holy standard isn't worthy of your affection. Holiness isn't just about saying no. It's also about saying yes—yes to worshiping together, learning together, and growing closer to God together. It's also good and right for you to enjoy your boyfriend's company and for you to have fun together.

DAY 96

"I will give you a new heart and put a new spirit in you; I will remove from you your heart of stone and give you a heart of flesh."

—EZEKIEL 36:26

It's easy to get the idea that the main difference between Christians and non-Christians is that Christians go to church. But did you know there's a real spiritual process that occurs when someone comes to saving faith? The theological term for it is "regeneration," and it's exactly what Ezekiel describes here.

If we're followers of Jesus, we've traded hearts of stone, hardened to God's love and his sovereignty in our lives, for hearts of flesh, sensitive to his Spirit, alive and beating and willing to be led by his Word. Our separateness—our differentness from those around us—is real. When God calls us to be set apart from those around us, he does so already having equipped us to run after his command.

Our new hearts twinge when we choose sin over holiness. Our new hearts grieve when we know we've driven a wedge between ourselves and God. Our new hearts long to live sin-free so that we might please God. When we're tempted to sin, we should remember the power of our flesh-heart, given to us by the God who enables us toward holiness.

DAY 97

"'This is the covenant I will make with the people of Israel after that time,' declares the LORD. 'I will put my law in their minds and write it on their hearts. I will be their God, and they will be my people.'"

—JEREMIAH 31:33

Most people who have read the Bible would agree that holiness is important to God. The sheer number of verses about it tell us that. But what standard do we use to figure out what holiness looks like?

God's law, recorded in Scripture, shows us his standard of what we're supposed to separate ourselves from. God's law is complex with several different types of laws. Some are ceremonial, like the sacrifices priests were supposed to offer for certain sins. Others are civil and were meant to show the Israelites how to run their rather unique government. These laws don't apply to the modern Christian who doesn't live under the ancient Israelite government and whose High Priest is Jesus Christ, the once-and-for-all sacrifice.

But the *moral* law is still active. When New Testament writers talk about following God's commands, these are the ones they mean. And Jeremiah prophesied that followers of Jesus would have the law inscribed on our minds and written on our hearts. The law lives within us, and if we allow our sensitive flesh-hearts to listen, God will help direct us toward greater holiness in him.

DAY 98

"You shall have no other gods before me."

—EXODUS 20:3

If we're looking to understand God's moral law, the Ten Commandments are a great place to start. If we've grown up going to Sunday school, we might have heard the commandments so many times, we don't really *hear* them anymore—at least not in a deep sense. Not in the sense that we're looking to uncover all the meanings of the words and apply them to our lives today, now. So let's change that.

We may think we're avoiding the "no other gods" commandment if we don't worship idols—and that's part of it. Idol worship is still a worldwide practice in some major religions and many tribal ones. But for those of us who live in countries or cultures where this practice is less common, what does "no other gods" mean?

In American culture, many people worship wealth, celebrity status, or power. Having money, being famous, and having power aren't bad, but the dogged pursuit and glorification of such things are. When we put these "gods" above the true God, we've lapsed into idolatry. Is there anything in your life you've been glorifying above God? Do some housecleaning and scrub that idol from your heart!

DAY 99

"You shall not make for yourself an image in the form of anything in heaven above or on the earth beneath or in the waters below."

—EXODUS 20:4

What's really at the heart of these first two commandments? Are physical idols the actual problem?

These commandments are so important and relevant to our lives because they shoot straight at a universal problem—where are we putting our trust? The Israelites veered off-course when they began to trust gods of wood and stone. The idea of an invisible God was downright strange in that culture.

Where are we putting our trust? Do we trust in a good job that will make lots of money? Are we trusting in our intelligence, our work ethic, or our talent? Are we trusting in our government? Relying on world leaders? It's not wrong to be confident in the abilities God gave us, and it's good to have trust built between people. But do we trust these worldly things above God?

God deserves the highest place of trust and honor in our lives. He gives us good gifts sometimes—stable governments, jobs that provide for our needs, enough money to cover our expenses and share with others—but if we don't acknowledge him as the source of these good things, it's easy to start putting our trust in the gifts, not the Giver.

DAY 100

"You shall not misuse the name of the LORD your God, for the LORD will not hold anyone guiltless who misuses his name."

—EXODUS 20:7

Misusing the name of the Lord is often interpreted to mean swearing using God's name. And while that's definitely something followers of Jesus should avoid, there's more to this commandment than what we see on the surface.

Words matter. They're powerful. The Bible says Jesus is the Word. We know salvation comes through hearing the word preached. God reveals himself to us through his Word. So it's important that we're mindful of our words, and especially the words we say about God.

Avoiding using God's name as a curse word is obvious. But let's broaden the definition of misusing God's name. How about using God's name in any way that dishonors him? This could be doing something wrong and saying it's for God, or that God commanded you to do it. Or it could be attributing something evil to God's hand. These are misuses of God's name that bring him dishonor. Is there an area in your life where you've misused God's name in some way? Can you use your words to bring him more honor and glorify him better?

DAY 101

"Remember the Sabbath day by keeping it holy. Six days you shall labor and do all your work, but the seventh day is a sabbath to the LORD your God."

—EXODUS 20:8–10

One day out of every week is to be set aside and kept holy—separate and dedicated to God. When life gets busy, the Sabbath can seem like a burden, yet another thing we *must* do. Lose an entire day out of the week because the Bible says so. But the Sabbath is really a blessing, and Jesus tells us that the Sabbath is for *us*. How sweet is it to have a day set aside from work and dedicated to worship, reflection, and service to God, especially in our busy lives?

Does this mean we shouldn't do *anything* on the Sabbath? No chores, no homework, no friends, no sports? We don't need to take it that far. The point of God's Sabbath isn't to burden his people; it's to bless them. We set aside time for God and time to hit "pause" on our busy lives.

So what can you do to better honor God with your Sabbaths? Is there a way to find more peaceful rest, deeper communion, more faithful service to the Lord? Pick one area and focus on it this week. Enjoy the gift of rest and dedicated time to God!

DAY 102

"Honor your father and your mother, so that you may live long in the land the Lord your God is giving you."

—EXODUS 20:12

Have you ever noticed that this commandment comes with a promise? God told the Israelites to honor their parents so that they may live long in the Promised Land. Today, we might not be living in the physical Promised Land, but the principle still applies. Honor your parents and it will be a blessing to you—and them.

What does honoring your parents look like? Obedience is an obvious factor. When they set a rule for you, obeying it is one way to honor them. But is outward obedience the only—or best—way to honor your parents? How do you speak of them when they're not around or to them when they are? If you honor them with your words and your actions, how about your heart? How is your attitude toward your parents?

This commandment may be straightforward, but that doesn't mean it's easy. Parents mess up. They're not perfect. But think about what you can do to approach your relationship with your parents in humility, openness, and grace. You might be surprised how rewarding it is.

DAY 103

"You shall not murder."

—EXODUS 20:13

It wouldn't be too surprising if the majority of readers skimmed over this commandment. Most of us take a glance, think "Yeah, haven't done that this week," and move right along to the next verse. In fact, on the surface, it might be the *easiest* commandment to follow. How often have you even had to resist the temptation to actually kill someone? Probably not very often.

But Jesus doesn't let us off that easy. While the law teaches us God's commands, Jesus always looks at the heart behind the command. The law says, "Don't kill," but the apostle John says whoever hates a brother or sister has already killed that person in her heart (1 John 3:15). Wow!

It's not enough to not physically kill someone. Jesus says our hearts are guilty of breaking this commandment if we've felt anger toward someone (Matthew 5:21–22). Has someone personally hurt you so deeply that you've hated them? Have you ever hated a terrorist group so much, you wish they would be wiped off the earth? Look deep in your heart and see if you're housing any hatred there. Release it. Forgive. Choose love, even for your enemies.

DAY 104

"You shall not commit adultery."

—EXODUS 20:14

Adultery is easily defined as sex that dishonors marriage vows. Most people know that if you're married, having sex with someone you're not married to is adultery. It's a serious offense. The Bible forbids sex outside of marriage in all contexts, but under the law, the punishments for adultery were the most severe.

Perhaps you're not married now, so this feels like it doesn't apply to you. But would you like to be married in the future? And if so, do you have an obligation to your future spouse to obey this command? What about someone you're dating? What if we're talking about kissing, not sex? Does this commandment apply to those situations too?

The real problem with adultery is that it destroys trust and intimacy, not to mention it dishonor's God's original design for sex. The heart of this commandment is that God wants his children to be people who show fidelity. That means waiting for marriage to have sex in order to honor God. It means not cheating on boyfriends, even "just" kissing. Make choices that reflect faithfulness to honor this commandment.

"You shall not steal."

—EXODUS 20:15

Thievery has no place in the life of a believer. That should seem obvious, and perhaps it is when we're talking about large things. Not too many Christians would try to put up a defense for stealing a car, breaking into someone's house and swiping jewelry, or knocking off a bank. And maybe it's obvious about smaller thefts, too, like shoplifting or swiping a twenty from your mom's wallet.

But some other types of theft might not be as obvious. What about being dishonest on your timesheet at work, saying you worked more hours than you did? Or have you ever pirated media or software? A lot of stolen music, books, movies, and software is available on the Internet. In the interest of keeping this commandment, Christians should hold to the highest standards of integrity, and that includes "harmless" theft or piracy.

"You shall not give false testimony against your neighbor."

—EXODUS 20:16

"Giving false testimony" could simply be summed up as lying. We know from many other verses in the Bible that God values truth and abhors lying. And this commandment specifically notes lying about others, which is not only wrong on principle, but it hurts another person. And you don't have to be on a witness stand, literally testifying, to spread untruth about others.

Avoiding gossip is one application of this command, especially when you're not sure if the gossip is even true. How about when you're having conflict with a friend? Sometimes it's tempting to stir up our mutual friends against the friend who has hurt or offended us, and in order to do that, it may be doubly tempting to gloss over a detail here or there to make our case more compelling. Giving in to that temptation lands you squarely in "false testimony" territory.

We should also be careful about what sort of media we share online. Sharing gossipy, heavily biased, or flat-out disproven news stories without doing research first can spread false testimony and make victims out of people we've never even met. Be careful with your words and actions!

DAY 107

"You shall not covet your neighbor's house. You shall not covet your neighbor's wife, or his male or female servant, his ox or donkey, or anything that belongs to your neighbor."

—EXODUS 20:17

Is there a single person on earth who hasn't experienced jealousy? We see a friend get into our dream college while we were rejected. We look at someone else's happy family and wonder why ours is filled with drama. Or we can't even stand to be around that one girl who gets the lead in every school play, scores the winning goal in every soccer game, and beats our GPA every semester. Maybe it seems like our parents always favor our siblings. Or we look at a rich person living a luxurious life and wonder why we've been given less.

Jealousy is about comparison. It's about taking a look at what you have, a look at what someone else has, and feeling like you've been cheated—like it's not fair. Like you deserve more. What's so wrong about it? Covetousness is the opposite of contentment and it acts as a very strong seed—like an acorn, it eventually grows into an oak tree. That oak tree is bitterness, and at the root of that tree is a lack of trust in God's good plan *for us.* Rest in God's plan—and God's timing—for your life to guard against jealousy.

"The acts of the flesh are obvious: sexual immorality, impurity and debauchery; idolatry and witchcraft; hatred, discord, jealousy, fits of rage, selfish ambition, dissensions, factions and envy; drunkenness, orgies, and the like. I warn you, as I did before, that those who live like this will not inherit the kingdom of God."

—GALATIANS 5:19–21

So does our list of "holy goals" end at the Ten Commandments? Nope! There are many more verses that make up Moses's law, in addition to our New Testament directives on holiness from Jesus, Paul, and other writers. This list from Galatians contains other behaviors and activities for followers of Jesus to avoid. In fact, Paul says these acts of the flesh are "obvious."

Because the law is now written on our hearts and we have the Spirit to guide us, it's important that we listen to that leading as we make our choices. If you feel uncomfortable with something, even if it's not specifically listed as sin in Scripture, avoid it. Why violate your conscience?

There's a delicate balance between Christian freedom and conscience, and sometimes we slip into the error of proclaiming something "sin" when really it just makes us personally uncomfortable. While we don't want to make that mistake, we should never feel swayed to do anything when we feel God is leading us in the other direction.

"Therefore, I urge you, brothers and sisters, in view of God's mercy, to offer your bodies as a living sacrifice, holy and pleasing to God—this is your true and proper worship."

—ROMANS 12:1

Humans are startlingly good at coming up with new ways to harm our bodies. Most of us eat food we know isn't the best for us, at least sometimes. And while we know food doesn't make us holy or unholy (see God's words to Peter in Acts), the Bible does note that our bodies are important. We're supposed to care for our bodies as an act of worship.

So what's off-limits for Jesus's followers? Drunkenness, or excessive drinking of alcohol, is warned against in both Testaments. It probably goes without saying that abusing drugs falls into this same category. Illegal drugs (and abuse of legal prescription drugs) are dangerous and extraordinarily harmful to our bodies, our relationships, and our spiritual lives.

But substances are only part of the picture. Have you ever struggled with an eating disorder, like anorexia? Do you know someone who cuts her own body to manage emotional pain? These behaviors are harmful to our bodies but they're usually symptoms of an underlying psychological problem. If you're suffering with any of these behaviors, please get help from a qualified Christian counselor or pastor. You're not alone! God wants to lead you to greater physical and emotional health.

DAY 110

"You are to be holy to me because I, the Lord, am holy, and I have set you apart from the nations to be my own."

—LEVITICUS 20:26

Holiness is a wiggly creature. It's strange how people seem to veer sharply in one direction or the other when it comes to holiness. Either we don't emphasize it enough and therefore our pursuit of lives pleasing to God is lukewarm, at best. Or we get so wrapped up in the pursuit of holiness, we create rules beyond what the Bible calls out as sin and we lapse into the same error the Pharisees did. Worst of all, sometimes we forget we're saved by grace alone and not our righteous works. We lose sight of the fact that without Jesus, we'd be more lost than lost.

To maintain balance in our pursuit of holiness and avoid all these errors, it's important to remember *why* we strive for holiness. God says we're to be holy because he is holy. *He* has set us apart, not because we're worthy in our works, but simply because it gave him glory to do so. Period. When we remember this, it should prompt us to seek lives worthy of the grace God has already extended and to be a strong example of that saving grace (not human judgment) to others.

DAY 111

"And [the seraphim] were calling to one another: 'Holy, holy, holy is the Lord Almighty; the whole earth is full of his glory.'"

—ISAIAH 6:3

We can waste a lot of time trying to impress people. Maybe that means seeking the latest fashion trends, the nicest car, the highest grades. And it doesn't end there. When we're caught up with trying to impress others, it follows us throughout all stages of our lives—the most Instagram-worthy wedding, the best husband, the biggest corner office in the building, the nicest house, the cutest kids.

It's important for followers of Jesus not to be sucked into this vortex of seeking worldly honor and glory for ourselves. It's not bad to try for good grades or to think your boyfriend is adorable or to dream of a great job. Those are all good things! But it's not where our worth lies. Our worth lies in our identities in Jesus, the Son of God. God is called the Most Holy One, the one who fills the earth with his glory. He is the ultimate standard of all things—beauty, worth, goodness, and holiness. We seek to honor him, not ourselves and our own accomplishments, in our lives because *he* is the one who is glorified and worthy.

DAY 112

"Speak to the entire assembly of Israel and say to them: 'Be holy because I, the Lord *your God, am holy.'"*

—LEVITICUS 19:2

Be holy because I am. Boom. It's that simple. God said it to the Israelites, and he says it to us. "Do this because it honors me. Do this because it reflects me. Do this because it's the way it was supposed to be in the beginning."

Simple, but not easy. Using God as our pattern for anything can feel overwhelming. He's so big. We're so small. How do we model ourselves after someone like God? If we squint really hard, we can maybe see his thumbprint on us, but . . . being holy like God? Is that even possible?

Of course, being perfectly holy like God is impossible in this life. But we're lucky. The Israelites may have had God's audible voice and visual presence, but we have Jesus. We have God *as a man* whose life we can study, whose words we can examine, whose footsteps we can try to follow. We can see what God looks like when cloaked in human flesh. In Christ, we have our ultimate example. How can you better walk like Jesus today?

DAY 113

"Make every effort to live in peace with everyone and to be holy; without holiness no one will see the Lord."

—HEBREWS 12:14

There's an unfortunate laziness that can be found sometimes in Jesus's followers who live in comfort. When it doesn't cost us much, physically or socially, to follow Jesus, it's easy to lapse into spiritual sluggishness. Christianity becomes routine. It's not a matter of life or death the way it is for some brothers and sisters around the world, so we forget. We forget how much we'd be willing to lay down for Jesus. We forget what our lives would be like without him.

But here the author of Hebrews says we're to make *every effort*. Every. Single. Effort. For both peace and holiness. And why is it so important? Is this verse saying that if we don't do these things, we'll lose our salvation? Thankfully, no. We know salvation is based on grace, not on our works. But our deeds as we strive, hard, after holiness are evidence of the salvation we've already received. Our outward expressions—words and deeds—show the change that's happened in our hearts. Gut-check time: Do your deeds show evidence of your heart? If not, consider why. We can pray for God to help us better reflect what he's done for us.

DAY 114

"They disciplined us for a little while as they thought best; but God disciplines us for our good, in order that we may share in his holiness."

—HEBREWS 12:10

Discipline isn't generally fun. Most of us learned this as toddlers when our moms and dads tried to parent those tantrums out of us. Or sometimes, as they struggled to keep us from seriously harming ourselves in our childish curiosity.

Discipline often involves punishment. When we were little, maybe that looked like timeout. When it's coming from God, it often looks like worldly consequences. Emotional fallout. Trouble with the law. Lost relationships. Missed opportunities. These are all things that can happen when we make ungodly choices.

And that discipline—consequences and correction—serves to get us back on course. We remember, "God doesn't want me to live this way for a reason. I need to get myself right with his wisdom again." We are shepherded back to the narrow path that leads toward holiness. Have you ever experienced God's discipline in your life before? He does that because he loves you! He wants you to grow in holiness and live a life pleasing to him.

DAY 115

"To make her [the church] holy, cleansing her by the washing with water through the word, and to present her to himself as a radiant church, without stain or wrinkle or any other blemish, but holy and blameless."

—EPHESIANS 5:26–27

Jesus's followers have a special call within the world. We're to be holy and blameless, radiant, as we're presented to God like a perfect bride. It's a pretty cool picture that shows us just how much God loves us, just how beautiful he thinks we are.

But there are also some serious implications here. Not only is each individual supposed to be growing in personal holiness, the whole church should be growing in holiness. Is that what we've seen in the global church? How about in the American church? Do we see a slow, steady increase in holiness . . . or do we see the opposite?

In areas of the world where Christians face intense persecution, we see a strong church, standing in conviction and holiness. We see Jesus's followers sacrificing their lives rather than denying their faith. But what about in areas where it's a little more comfortable to be a Christian? Where it doesn't cost quite as much to follow Jesus?

It's important that we keep this on our radar. If the church, at large, isn't growing in holiness, we're missing something. Make every effort to be part of the change!

DAY 116

"Fix these words of mine in your hearts and minds; tie them as symbols on your hands and bind them on your foreheads. Teach them to your children, talking about them when you sit at home and when you walk along the road, when you lie down and when you get up. Write them on the doorframes of your houses and on your gates . . ."

—DEUTERONOMY 11:18–20

If the global church, or the church in our nation, isn't growing in holiness the way it should, we need to rise up and change that. Every generation has the opportunity to make a real impact. But how? How do we, as an entire community, move in that direction?

One of the biggest, best things we can do is by making God's words a priority in our churches and our lives. It's easy to be swayed by the world, swayed by culture, when we don't have our feet planted firmly in the Bible. The Bible—not culture, not politics, not media, not even books *about* the Bible—should be our final standard on everything. God's call to the Israelites here still resonates today. Fix these words—his law—on our hearts and minds. Know them backwards and forwards. Let them infuse every part of our personal lives and our church lives.

When we truly *live* the word, there's no way to grow except in holiness.

DAY 117

"Seek good, not evil, that you may live. Then the Lord *God Almighty will be with you, just as you say he is."*

—AMOS 5:14

The church should always seek after the good. It may not seem so at first, but there's a difference between merely sidestepping evil and actually going after the good.

Imagine you're on a path. There are landmines everywhere, each one marked with a little flag. You know just where *not* to step, so you tiptoe through, avoiding the flagged bombs. But what if there were little jewels along the way—sparkly gems you could reach down and pick up as you avoided the landmines? Those jewels are like the good things we should be seeking and the landmines are the evil things we're supposed to avoid. It's entirely possible to simply avoid the bombs without picking up any jewels. But that's not God's complete plan for his church.

Maybe we've avoided falling into sin and error, but are we loving people the way we're called to? Are we doing all the good the church is supposed to do? A church that looks like Jesus is one that avoids sin while personifying God's love.

DAY 118

"Get rid of all bitterness, rage and anger, brawling and slander, along with every form of malice."

—EPHESIANS 4:31

The Internet is a pretty cool invention. It allows us to stay connected like never before. We can find people of similar interests, no matter how small a niche our hobbies fall into. We have the potential to be exposed to new ideas, multiple sides of an issue, experts on many topics. Most of the information the world has to offer is right there, one Google search away. And all without changing out of our pajamas.

But often, the Internet isn't used like this—even amongst the church. The fighting in the comments of Christian publications and blogs is just as bad, if not worse, than what you'd find on a secular news article. It's okay to feel passionate about topics like doctrine or Christian living. But the lack of unity amongst Jesus's followers is truly distressing. Name-calling, salvation-questioning, and the word "heresy" appear an awful lot. And this is the witness presented to unbelievers silently watching the comment stream.

Jesus's followers will be known by their unity and love. While doctrinal purity is important, we can encourage the church toward holiness by seeking unity and peace and avoiding excessive infighting and needless controversy with our fellow brothers and sisters.

DAY 119

"Do not forget the covenant I have made with you."

—2 KINGS 17:38A

Life gets busy. We get distracted, overwhelmed, worn out. It's easy to forget our calling, to forget our special relationship with God and how he calls us to holiness. And sometimes, when we know we're going our own way and rebelling against God, we *want* to forget.

But it's vital we don't forget. It's vital we continue, even when times are tough and we feel like we have no energy for holiness. Why? Because our lives are like living signposts, pointing others toward Jesus. You may think you're not an evangelist because you're shy or uncomfortable speaking to others about your faith. But everything you do is evangelism. Growing and acting in faith, wisdom, and holiness is your living witness.

Take a hard look at your life, as it stands today. Are you a signpost pointing toward Jesus, or are you pointing toward something else? If you think you might be pointing more clearly toward something other than Jesus, don't panic! God can and will help you turn it around, if you ask.

"King David dedicated these articles to the LORD, as he had done with the silver and gold from all the nations he had subdued."

—2 SAMUEL 8:11

This verse is a great one to support the principle of tithing—giving a portion of the money you earn back to the church for God's service (which is a very good principle to practice). But there's another spiritual truth within these words: We are the silver and gold articles dedicated to the Lord!

Our "walking signpost" lives are set apart, called holy, by God. We exist for God's pleasure and his glory. He plucked us out of whatever life we'd be living without him and said, "Her. This one. She belongs to me. I've set her apart for holy purposes."

Think about how God has set you apart for himself. When we're able to wrap our minds around this idea—and sometimes, that's a challenge—it's hard not to realize how utterly adored we are. God didn't need us, but he chose us. Walk in holiness and with purpose!

DAY 121

"On that day holy to the LORD will be inscribed on the bells of the horses, and the cooking pots in the LORD's house will be like the sacred bowls in front of the altar. Every pot in Jerusalem and Judah will be holy to the LORD Almighty, and all who come to sacrifice will take some of the pots and cook in them. And on that day there will no longer be a Canaanite in the house of the LORD Almighty."

—ZECHARIAH 14:20–21

The final completion of holiness will come when eternity does. It'd be so awesome to be able to get there wholly in this life, but we're going to mess up. We're going to make mistakes and some bad choices. That's why we cling so desperately to our savior—why we're so thankful that our salvation doesn't depend on our perfection but on *his*.

The perfect holiness of eternity will show us a newly created world the way God had always planned it. No sin, no imperfection to mar it. We won't be pulled by selfishness, pride, greed, or hatred anymore. It will only be all praise to God, all the time. Joy!

Looking forward to this perfectly holy eternity spent with our creator can inspire us in this lifetime too. Let's let the promise of that future pure joy propel us to do all God has called us to here and now. We have a whole lot to look forward to!

DAY 122

"And he passed in front of Moses, proclaiming, 'The LORD, the LORD, the compassionate and gracious God, slow to anger, abounding in love and faithfulness.'"

—EXODUS 34:6

When we focus on the holy perfection of God, it's easy to be terrified of him. I mean . . . he's God. He's big, powerful, and has a zero-tolerance policy for sin, which is something we do every day. That sounds like a recipe for the human race getting zapped off the planet pretty quickly.

And yet, here we are. Not zapped. That's because there is more to God's character than his complete and perfect holiness. God's goodness exists alongside his holiness. And the intensity of God's goodness mirrors the intensity of his holiness.

God's goodness is so vast, it can be broken down into three specific traits: his mercy, his grace, and his patience. Today, let's rejoice that our perfectly holy God is also our perfectly good God who shows us compassion, grace, and patience.

"Grace, mercy and peace from God the Father and from Jesus Christ, the Father's Son, will be with us in truth and love."

—2 JOHN 3

When we feel like we've failed, it's easy to wonder why God would "waste" his goodness on us. We may ask God why he would choose someone so small and weak to be called his daughter.

But the truth is that even when we're doing our best to meet God's standards, we still don't measure up. Our efforts have nothing to do with why God chooses us. God has grace because he chooses to. God shows mercy because he wants to. God is patient because it's who he is.

In turn, we're expected to show the face of God to the rest of the world. God's goodness fills us up from the inside out, and we shine truth and love to all who don't know God yet. We get to serve as God's ambassadors to a world that has rejected him—or hasn't even met him yet. It's a big responsibility! Consider how you can shine more of God's truth and love into others' lives today.

DAY 124

"Dear friend, do not imitate what is evil but what is good. Anyone who does what is good is from God. Anyone who does what is evil has not seen God."

—3 JOHN 11

The apostle John was Jesus's best friend on earth. He was an awesome writer, but he was also a writer of extremes. It's John who tells us that if we claim to have a relationship with God but continue to walk with in darkness, we're liars (1 John 1:6). And here, John tells us that anyone who neglects doing good to do evil hasn't even *seen* God. Wow!

Though they may sound extreme, John's words can't be discounted. Sometimes these strong statements are what we need to jolt us from complacency and ask ourselves, "Am I living the way a child of light is supposed to? Am I reflecting God to the world? How can I do better?"

Once again, John shows us the standard for God's people—a lifestyle of goodness. It doesn't mean the occasional good deed or random act of kindness. It means the day in, day out loving of others. Make a habit of chasing after the good, and you'll find yourself on the right side of John's extremes.

DAY 125

"David said to Gad, 'I am in deep distress. Let us fall into the hands of the Lord, for his mercy is great; but do not let me fall into human hands.'"

—2 SAMUEL 24:14

The Bible has a lot to say about God's mercy, and mercy is defined as God's goodness to those who are in misery and distress.

Have you ever felt miserable or distressed? Most of us have, whether due to something outside our control or as a result of our own faults and failures. In these times, it's easy to feel alone, forgotten, and unloved. It's easy to imagine that God has abandoned us.

But God's Word shows us the truth. God does not abandon those who are in misery or distress. In fact, he holds his hands out beneath us, ready to catch us as we fall. King David, who often found himself in positions of great distress, knew this truth. He often prayed to fall on God's great mercy—both when he was the one in error and when he was fleeing for his life through no fault of his own. Like David, we can rest in God's mercy and his care for the distressed.

DAY 126

"And everyone who calls on the name of the LORD will be saved; for on Mount Zion and in Jerusalem there will be deliverance, as the LORD has said, even among the survivors whom the LORD calls."

—JOEL 2:32

Every human being experiences spiritual distress, whether she knows it or not. Our sin separates us from God. Our souls hang in the balance. It sounds terrifying—hopeless, even.

But God's greatest mercy to humankind is what Jesus calls his "easy yoke" (Matthew 11:30). That term may sound strange to our modern ears. Trust me, it has nothing to do with an egg (that's a yolk). A yoke is what's placed over the shoulders of oxen to attach them to the carts or plows they pull. So when Jesus said his yoke was easy, he was saying the burden he would place on the shoulders of those wishing to come to the father through him would be light.

As Joel prophesied, all we have to do is call on the name of the Lord. That's it. Instead of facing a hopeless situation of trying to measure up to a standard we can't reach, God, in his mercy, has allowed us free access to him, if only we believe and call on his name. That's worth celebrating!

DAY 127

"In my distress I called to the LORD, and he answered me. From deep in the realm of the dead I called for help, and you listened to my cry."

—JONAH 2:2

There are 7.4 billion people on the planet. That's a lot of people. It seems incredible that we're even able to fit on earth's land, with room to spare.

And yet, despite the sheer number of humans shuffling over the earth's surface, every single cry of distress is heard by God. Every prayer offered in misery is heard and answered, even when it doesn't feel like it.

Sometimes our answer is "No," or "Not now," or "Wait a little longer." Sometimes we get a loud "Yes!" and relief comes immediately. Other times, God is still working out his good plan. But we can be sure that God is always listening. We can lean into his mercy. We can find peace in the fact that our God has a heart for the distressed. He is with us, no matter what our current circumstances look like.

DAY 128

"Listen, my dear brothers and sisters: Has not God chosen those who are poor in the eyes of the world to be rich in faith and to inherit the kingdom he promised those who love him?"

—JAMES 2:5

If God has a special heart of mercy for the distressed and miserable, we should too. James's writings show us how God often looks past the worldly things we tend to get caught up in. He doesn't see riches and worldly honor when selecting his children. He doesn't look at how physically attractive a person is, how popular they are, or how strong.

In fact, the Bible tells us that God often chooses the poor, the weak, and the broken to accomplish his purposes. There is special mercy shown to the ones who don't look like the champions the world would choose.

We can ask God to give us *his* eyes to see past the things that matter to the world. We can ask God to help us see hearts the way he does. In looking deeper toward people's hearts, we will better love the distressed, just like our God does.

DAY 129

"He has shown you, O mortal, what is good. And what does the Lord require of you? To act justly and to love mercy and to walk humbly with your God."

—MICAH 6:8

How do Christians look different from the rest of the world? Is it that we go to church on Sunday, always have a Bible nearby, and we know all the songs in the hymnal (or projected onto the big screen, if you're fancy like that) by heart? Those are all great things, and we should go to church, read our Bibles, and sing worship songs to God. But the Bible goes a little deeper than that.

The mark of a believer isn't even how quickly she can quote scripture, how many times she's volunteered in the church nursery, or how well she cleans up after church events without complaining (though that level of service surely deserves special mention). No, the Bible says the Lord requires us to act with justice, to love mercy, and to walk humbly. Simple, but not always easy!

"You will be enriched in every way so that you can be generous on every occasion, and through us your generosity will result in thanksgiving to God."

—2 CORINTHIANS 9:11

God's great mercy to us empowers us to show generosity to others. When we use the word "generosity," we often think of money. And that is definitely one area where Christians should be generous. When we recognize all our financial blessings come from God, it's easy to share them with others. We receive and then should give with an open hand.

But there are other ways to show generosity. Giving time and energy is a huge help to others. Sometimes this means volunteering at church, school, or charities. But it can also be on a one-on-one basis. Maybe there's someone in your life who seems lonely. Maybe you have a friend who is going through a really tough time. Can you be her listening ear? Can you make a point to check in with her? Sometimes our caring attention is a lifeline for someone who is struggling.

Be generous with your money, time, and love. That generosity reflects the mercy we've received from God. Be a light to someone in need!

DAY 131

"Command those who are rich in this present world not to be arrogant nor to put their hope in wealth, which is so uncertain, but to put their hope in God, who richly provides us with everything for our enjoyment."

—1 TIMOTHY 6:17

Everything in our culture tells us to trust in wealth. It's okay to be wise about saving and spending our money—in fact, it's a good thing! We should be responsible with everything God entrusts to us, and that includes money. But when wealth becomes our main focus, we've crossed the line into an unhealthy zone.

Being wealthy also tempts us toward arrogance. When we're arrogant, we are relying on ourselves and our own awesomeness, not God's provision and *his* awesomeness. This verse in 1 Timothy tells us God provides everything for our enjoyment. He does that because of his goodness.

Are we using his rich provisions in this world in ways that honor him? Are we enjoying those provisions, or putting our faith in them? Do a heart-check and make sure you're using the blessings of our merciful God in the best way possible.

"Be merciful to those who doubt."

—JUDE 22

Be kind to those who share your faith and despise those who don't. That's what the Bible says, right? No? Uh-oh . . .

If we were just looking at how people correspond on the Internet, it would be easy to get the idea that the Bible *does* say this somewhere. But it doesn't. Instead, Jude gives us a strong statement in the opposite direction—be merciful to those who doubt. That's not an easy directive. It feels much more natural to show contempt for those who reject our faith or who are unsure about God and this whole Christianity deal.

But, once again, the Bible asks us to go against our first instincts. Show goodness—love and mercy—to those who doubt. Show tender care to those who are searching but unsure. God loves these lost sheep, just like he loved us before we discovered him.

"A bruised reed he will not break, and a smoldering wick he will not snuff out. In faithfulness he will bring forth justice."

—ISAIAH 42:3

Distress is relative. For some people, distress is an important test they didn't do well on. For others, distress is embarrassing themselves in front of friends (or worse, frenemies). Or for someone else, distress might be having lied to a parent and now needing to come clean (gulp).

God cares about each of those situations. And they are distressing, certainly. But what about when our distressing situations are deeper and more volatile than that? What if distress looks like emotional or sexual abuse? What if we're talking about physical violence?

First, talk to someone you trust. Don't stay silent if you're experiencing abuse. Get help from a parent, pastor, teacher, friend, counselor, or police officer, if appropriate. Also know that you are so adored by God. We don't always get to know why we find ourselves in certain situations, but we do know that God loves "bruised reeds" and he will sustain us through our deepest, most painful distress.

DAY 134

"The Lord is close to the brokenhearted and saves those who are crushed in spirit."

—PSALM 34:18

There's no shortage of pain in our world. Around the globe, people suffer in ways a lot of us can't imagine. Lack of food, clean water, and proper medicines are daily realities in some regions. In some areas, war and violence are the norm. Other have oppressive governments that don't allow their citizens freedom.

And even in our relatively rich, privileged country, suffering abounds. Sometimes it's physical, sometimes it's emotional. Incurable medical conditions, broken homes, substance abuse. All of us have experienced some level of suffering. It's the reality of a world that has been broken by sin.

But God stays close to us in our painful times. He never ventures far when we're in misery. God's goodness moves him to have a special outpouring of mercy to the brokenhearted. If you're brokenhearted now, know that God is beside you. If you know someone who is brokenhearted right now, show her God's love by being near.

DAY 135

"For our light and momentary troubles are achieving for us an eternal glory that far outweighs them all."

—2 CORINTHIANS 4:17

It can be hard to read the words "light and momentary troubles" when we're experiencing some really heavy, really serious stuff. But when the apostle Paul wrote these words, he had experienced severe hardship in several places along his missionary journeys. It's not like he had lived a cushy life and didn't know what true hardship looked like.

And still, he calls our earthly trials "light and momentary." Still he says our trials are refining us for a glory that outweighs in good anything bad we experience during our lives.

When we suffer, especially as a result of someone else's sin, it does not mean that God has left us. It does not mean God has forgotten us. God is still near, and our future with him is always secure.

DAY 136

"For the entire law is fulfilled in keeping this one command: 'Love your neighbor as yourself.'"

—GALATIANS 5:14

It's a big, wide world out there. It's not always easy to navigate interacting with people who are different—throughout the world and also in our own neighborhoods. It can be hard to find common ground if we don't share culture, language, religion, or heritage. How can we learn to overcome differences and treat people the way God wants us to?

If you guessed something about returning to God's Word, you get a gold star. In fact, take twenty of them. How often we forget to do this! And the Bible states things so simply for us: love your neighbor as yourself. That's what God's mercy looks like.

Regardless of how each of our governments choose to act, we can take up this call as individuals. So who are these neighbors we're supposed to love? Who are the ones the Bible calls us to show mercy to? The oppressed, the alien, the refugee, the widow (single parents), the orphan (kids in foster care). What is one concrete way you can help one of these people God has shown special care toward? Look into a ministry that serves one of these groups and ask them what they need!

DAY 137

"Carry each other's burdens, and in this way you will fulfill the law of Christ."

—GALATIANS 6:2

Racial tension is a difficult, complex topic in our culture right now. Some groups feel they're not being heard, respected, or treated decently. Other groups feel they're unfairly seen as villains. Other groups don't have any clue what to do or how to help, so they stay silent.

Racial tension is nothing new, and it's never easy for a society to heal wounds of this nature. So where does that leave people who love Jesus? What's our role? As recipients of God's mercy, we should be the ones leading the charge toward love and compassion.

Christians have a specific call to carry the burdens of others. How well are we fulfilling that call? Are we leading the charge with love, or are we refusing to listen? Respond with compassion. Show God's love. Be part of the solution.

DAY 138

"He was despised and rejected by mankind, a man of suffering, and familiar with pain. Like one from whom people hide their faces he was despised, and we held him in low esteem."

—ISAIAH 53:3

Jesus was familiar with rejection. He was familiar with being an outcast. He was dishonored in his hometown, as those who had watched him grow up in a normal family had an impossible time accepting the idea that he might be the Messiah. Even worse, he was wholly abandoned (at least temporarily) by all his friends at the moment he needed them most—just as he was sent to the cross. And while he was on the cross, fulfilling his ultimate purpose, he even cried out to God, asking why he'd been forgotten.

Jesus has a special heart for the outcast and a special love for the rejected. Maybe you feel like you don't fit in or like no one understands you. Maybe friends or family have abandoned you because of your faith. Jesus is close to you in these moments.

Even if you've never felt like an outcast personally, it's pretty certain you've known someone who has felt that way. Pay attention to the rejected ones. Show Jesus's love to those who need it most.

DAY 139

"For all have sinned and fall short of the glory of God, and all are justified freely by his grace through the redemption that came by Christ Jesus."

—ROMANS 3:23–24

Grace is a word we hear and read a lot, especially in the New Testament. Sometimes, we become "word-blind" to these common bits of Christianese. We skim them as we read and don't really take the time to reflect on their deep truths. So what is the real meaning of this common Bible word, grace?

Grace is God's goodness to those who deserve punishment. And, not to bum anyone out, but "those who deserve punishment" is all of us. We've all failed to live up to God's standard many, many times, and even just one sin is enough to owe God our lives. Gulp.

But that's why this word—grace—is used so frequently by the New Testament writers. That's why Paul's letters mention it over and over. It is by God's grace—his goodness to us when we don't deserve it—that we are able to be saved. The entire Gospel message rests on God's grace.

DAY 140

"Be kind and compassionate to one another, forgiving each other, just as in Christ God forgave you."

—EPHESIANS 4:32

When we talk about grace, most of the time we're talking about spiritual forgiveness. Because God is good, he chooses to forgive his children instead of punish them. That's who he is. He chooses to look on Jesus's sinless life and death and accept that as *our* payment for our sins.

Have you ever stopped to think how adored you are? God loved you so much, he allowed his only son to suffer and die so that he could show us grace and fulfill his law. That's next-level love. Talk to anyone with children and they'll tell you that losing one of their kids is the worst possible thing they can imagine. And our human kids aren't even perfect! But still, parents would sacrifice just about anything to keep their kids well and safe.

But God didn't withhold his son. Jesus's life, death, and resurrection was the only way to complete God's plan for salvation. God orchestrated it, and Jesus was obedient to it—even though we can never do enough to earn it. How deeply loved we are to be the recipients of such grace!

DAY 141

"May God give you heaven's dew and earth's richness— an abundance of grain and new wine."

—GENESIS 27:28

Though we're usually talking about spiritual forgiveness when we discuss the word grace, there are other kinds of grace too. God shows spiritual grace to his children, but he shows his love for all mankind through what's called "common grace." Common grace is a fancy theological term for the good things that come from God regardless of whether we have faith or not.

What! I know, but think about it. Even the most adamant enemy of God gets air to breathe. He may even get a long, healthy life on earth. We all get sunshine and rain. We all get land to grow crops or raise animals (or we live in places where we're privileged enough to buy these things at the grocery store without the hard work of growing them ourselves).

Even people who wholly reject God their entire lives experience some measure of God's grace. His love for humanity extends to each person, and sometimes, this common grace becomes the starting point of recognizing God's goodness and coming to saving faith and spiritual grace!

DAY 142

"Moreover, when God gives someone wealth and possessions, and the ability to enjoy them, to accept their lot and be happy in their toil—this is a gift of God."

—ECCLESIASTES 5:19

Sometimes God shows us grace in the form of material blessings. We don't necessarily deserve any of the things God gives to us, but he's pleased to do so anyway. That is a direct result of his gracious goodness.

So how are we supposed to respond? In a materially wealthy culture, it's easy to become really fixated on our possessions. When we do, our blessings feel more like curses. Whatever we have, it's never big enough, new enough, fancy enough, or good enough. We enter into an endless cycle of trying to outdo ourselves and others. Yuck.

Instead, we should focus on two words when we think of God's gracious material blessings: thankfulness and generosity. When we remain in an attitude of thankfulness, we keep our focus on the Giver, not the gifts. When the gifts aren't our focus, it becomes easier to share our material wealth with others. Thank God for his good gifts today, and consider how you might show generosity to someone in need.

DAY 143

"For it is by grace you have been saved, through faith—and this is not from yourselves, it is the gift of God."

—EPHESIANS 2:8

Sometimes God's plans befuddle us. In fact, God's plans often befuddle us. In Ancient Israel's time, the idea of a wholly invisible God with no physical idol to represent him was strange and novel. So much so that the Israelites, though they had seen with their own eyes the mighty power of God, often fell prey to worshiping lifeless gods of wood and stone.

And these days, we have the novel concept of grace. Most religions are filled with rituals and lists, so to speak, of all the things a faithful follower must do to uphold the tenets of that religion. But Christianity is different. It's almost too easy! Just believe in Jesus's sacrifice, and you're saved. That's it. What a strange plan for salvation!

But God's good plan keeps the believer spiritually humble. We're continually pointed back to the fact that we didn't earn our salvation. Jesus did. We're continually pointed back to the fact that we didn't deserve God's love. We deserved punishment. But God withheld it because it pleased him, not because we're particularly awesome. Let's thank God today—for his grace, and for keeping us from spiritual arrogance.

DAY 144

"For this reason I remind you to fan into flame the gift of God, which is in you through the laying on of my hands."

—2 TIMOTHY 1:6

Do you ever take a look at yourself—at all the areas where you feel inadequate or at all the times you've failed—and wonder why God would choose you? Don't worry. You're not alone. All of us feel that way sometimes. All of us find ourselves, at one point or another, saying, "Really, God? Why me?"

God shows that unearned grace to us so that we can turn around and show it to others. He breathes spiritual life into us and ignites the gifts inside of us so we can serve as his hands and feet on earth, bringing even more people into his grace.

God didn't make a mistake when he showed you grace. Just as there were likely those in your life who helped lead you to Christ, you are part of God's plan for someone else. Whose path can you light today?

DAY 145

"For you know the grace of our Lord Jesus Christ, that though he was rich, yet for your sake he became poor, so that you through his poverty might become rich."

—2 CORINTHIANS 8:9

Jesus-level grace requires sacrifice. It's hard for us to admit that sometimes. It's hard for us to step out of our comfort zones, give up things we think are important, or experience persecution. But often God calls us to do just that in the name of loving others.

Think about the most important thing in your life. Are you willing to give it up to follow Jesus? Are you willing to sacrifice your comfort so others might be saved? Ouch. It hurts to even think about it, doesn't it? In his goodness, God often lets us stay comfortable while serving him, not asking us to make really tough choices.

But are we willing if he does ask for that kind of sacrifice? Pray that your heart will be sensitive to the special tasks God may be asking of you, now or in the future. Respond in faith!

DAY 146

"The Lord is compassionate and gracious, slow to anger, abounding in love."

—PSALM 103:8

A lot of people have the idea that God is a big man in the sky with a fistful of lightning bolts, ready and waiting for people to make mistakes so he can zap them. That's the pop culture image of God, anyway. And sometimes, even Christians are perfectly willing to accept the God of the New Testament, fully revealed in Jesus Christ, but think of the Old Testament God as angry and vengeful.

It's true that God is holy. It's true that God describes himself as "jealous." And it's true that God does sometimes administer justice and punishment. But even in the Old Testament, God is described as "slow to anger." Not a Zeus-like figure storming around heaven, waiting to toss a bolt. Slow to anger. Patient. Absorbing the offenses done against him over long periods of time, not retaliating every chance we give him.

God's patience is evident all throughout the Bible, and it's evident today. Even as the world falls deeper and deeper into sin, Jesus waits to return and administer final judgment until everyone has heard his offer of salvation. Slow to anger, patient with our failures—that's the goodness of God.

DAY 147

"But the fruit of the Spirit is love, joy, peace, forbearance, kindness, goodness, faithfulness, gentleness and self-control. Against such things there is no law."

—GALATIANS 5:22–23

Has anyone ever described you as hot-tempered? Short-fused? Quick-tempered? Fiery? If so, you're definitely not alone. When someone hurts, annoys, or crosses us, it's difficult to keep control of the fire sometimes. In fact, our natural instincts will often tend toward anger or defensiveness.

But forbearance, which is a synonym for patience, is listed as part of the fruit of the Spirit. It's right up there beside love, joy, and peace. So this must be a pretty important attribute of God for us to emulate.

Think of concrete ways to help yourself grow in patience. Count to ten before responding to someone who has offended you. Take deep breaths. When experiencing conflict, pause to think of where you might have gone wrong instead of blaming the other person. Apologize for your shortcomings instead of pointing out the shortcomings of others. Practicing patience may feel like we're going against the grain—because we are—but it's worth it. Along with patience comes deeper relationships, greater peace, and less stress.

DAY 148

"But if we hope for what we do not yet have, we wait for it patiently."

—ROMANS 8:25

It's not easy to wait. We like to think we've come a long way since preschool, but when we're told we have to wait for something we *really* want, that inner Cookie Monster resurfaces. "Me want cookie! Nom-nom! Cookie, now!"

But when we're fully followers of Jesus, practicing patience isn't just a matter of maturity—it's a spiritual necessity. One of our greatest shows of faith is accepting God's timing in our lives. In patience and faith, we believe he is working his ultimate plan for our good.

It's not easy. Not even a little. But accepting God's timing will always work in our favor. He has the big picture. We have our Cookie-Monster wants and needs. He cares about each of his little Cookie Monsters, but he always knows what's best for us. Give up your deepest desires to God, and go where he leads, when he leads you.

DAY 149

"And as for you, brothers and sisters, never tire of doing what is good."

—2 THESSALONIANS 3:13

Discouragement is like a rude party-crasher. The guy who wasn't invited but shows up anyway and trashes the house, then leaves without cleaning up. No one wants or needs discouragement, and yet it shows up in each of our lives at some point. Sometimes this discouragement is about something personal—doors that seem to be closing in our faces, not being able to see the next step in God's plan, or even feeling like we're stuck in a rut.

Other times, discouragement comes on a larger, more global scale, as we watch our culture or our world go off the rails. How can we help? How do we fix it? Can one small person make any difference?

The Bible tells us never to tire of what is good. Never. We may not see how our one small action can make a difference in a global problem. Or we may feel like giving up when things aren't going well for us personally. But if we believe that God's plan will be fulfilled, it's important that we play our part. Keep pressing forward. Keep doing good. Fight discouragement!

"Be completely humble and gentle; be patient, bearing with one another in love."

—EPHESIANS 4:2

Completely humble and gentle? Sure, no problem! Done! Ahem.

This is a tall order. There's nothing easy about representing Jesus to the world, no matter how badly we want to do just that. But we need to realize how important it is. Our lives are living, breathing advertisements for Jesus and his church. What are we advertising to the world? Is it humility, gentleness, patience, and love? Or is it arrogance, harshness, and anger?

Church culture change starts with individuals. What can you do to refine and polish your testimony to the world? Are there areas where you need to grow in humility, gentleness, patience, or love? Pick one spot and focus on it. Then pick another and another. You can be the example, regardless of your age or how new you are to the church. Live out your faith!

DAY 151

"Therefore encourage one another and build each other up, just as in fact you are doing."

—1 THESSALONIANS 5:11

It's always easier to tear down than it is to build up. It's always easier to be negative than it is to be positive. It's always easier to criticize something than it is to create something.

But the Bible tells us to build each other up. Positivity, encouragement, and patience can go a long way in showing love to others. It's no secret that life isn't all rainbows, unicorns, kittens, and glitter (even if it should be, because glitter!). But that doesn't mean we shouldn't be a bright spot of light to others.

Think of ways that you can share some positivity today. Whose day can you brighten? Who can you encourage? Who can you build up? Spread some sparkle today, glitter appreciated though not required. (But probably leave your unicorn at home.)

"Do not worship any other god, for the LORD, whose name is Jealous, is a jealous God."

—EXODUS 34:14

Our God's name is Jealous. Uh . . . what? Isn't jealously a bad thing? Aren't we warned against being jealous? How can God be jealous?

This is another one of those words that, when applied to God, doesn't mean what we're used to it meaning. When the Bible describes God as being jealous, it means that God continuously seeks to protect his own honor. He is jealous for his name, his people, and his reputation.

God is on guard. He knows how he is spoken about and thought of. He knows how he is treated in public and in the individual's heart. And this aspect of his character—his jealousy—will continue to fight against misconceptions, misunderstandings, and flat-out rebellion. While the word "jealousy" brings to mind a negative picture for us, it's actually a wonderful aspect of God's character. He protects his name and, by extension, ours.

DAY 153

"For my own sake, for my own sake, I do this. How can I let myself be defamed? I will not yield my glory to another."

—ISAIAH 48:11

At first glance, this jealousy thing might feel like a double standard. God's very name is described as Jealous, but the Bible strictly warns us against jealousy. Not fair!

Except . . . he's God. His jealousy isn't the same as ours. When we're jealous, it's usually over something material. Maybe we're jealous that the guy who has caught our eye seems more into our best friend (ouch). Or maybe we're jealous when a friend gets a brand-new car for her sixteenth birthday and we're still driving our mom's station wagon when she's not using it (and don't forget to fill it up before you return it to her). Our jealousy is centered around wanting something we don't have. God's jealousy, in line with his perfect holiness, seeks to protect his own name and our very souls. God's jealousy is the opposite of green-eyed envy. Like everything about God, it comes from his perfect love.

"Now if you obey me fully and keep my covenant, then out of all nations you will be my treasured possession."

—EXODUS 19:5A

So, what does God have to be jealous about? When the Bible speaks about God's jealousy, it is very often connected to the way God feels about his people—Ancient Israel in the Old Testament and his church in the New Testament. And that's because we're his treasured possession.

"Treasured" is such a great word. It brings to mind God holding his people close—tenderly and lovingly guarding us. We belong to him, and he wants to protect us. He wants to bless us, to grow us, and to mold us to look more like his son. That's a big truth. How would it change the way we move through life if we could, every minute of every day, remember that we are God's adored, beloved, treasured people?

DAY 155

"For this is what the Sovereign Lord says: I myself will search for my sheep and look after them."

—EZEKIEL 34:11

Have you ever known anyone who seemed to be part of God's flock, only to wander away and seem lost forever? Maybe you've been that person. Maybe you had faith once but lately you feel filled with doubt or like God has left you.

Don't be afraid. God's love is big. It's big enough to bring back those who wander. Each person matters to him. Each sheep is a treasured possession, and he will earnestly seek those who belong to him. God's name and God's honor matter to him. If we're part of his flock, he seeks to protect his name and his honor by bringing us back.

Sheep can be willful and stubborn, just like God's people. But God is always calling, always ready to accept lost sheep. If you've been feeling like a lost sheep, return to him now. He's waiting. If you know a lost sheep, pray for her or him. God adores his treasured flock.

DAY 156

"For you are a people holy to the L*ORD your God. Out of all the peoples on the face of the earth, the* L*ORD has chosen you to be his treasured possession."*

—DEUTERONOMY 14:2

God's treasured possessions—his people—are a "holy" people. We've examined that word pretty closely already, and one of the definitions of holy means "set apart." That's what we are: a people set apart for God.

That means we're different. Sometimes this is a great thing, like when the world knows us because we're showing compassion to those in distress or because we seek to bring peace or joy or love to difficult situations. In those moments, it's great to be different! Sometimes it's painful. When people reject our Savior or scorn our God, it's difficult to be different. It hurts to be God's treasured possession in those moments, because we are able to see truths others aren't, and that's disheartening and frustrating.

It also means we're dedicated to him. We don't seek after our own desires and our own glory in the same way the world does. We seek after God's desires for us (which are awesome!) and seek to glorify him, not ourselves, in our lives. Embrace your status as different, dedicated, and treasured by God. Keeping this identity close to our hearts helps us to fulfil God's commands without shrinking away from others' judgments.

DAY 157

"Then he took the Book of the Covenant and read it to the people. They responded, 'We will do everything the LORD has said; we will obey.'"

—EXODUS 24:7

Being God's treasured possessions means we're in a covenant relationship with him. Covenant what?! I know, "covenant" sounds like church-speak these days, but it wasn't back in the Old Testament. Covenants in the Old Testament were like modern-day contracts—legal agreements that outline what each signing person is agreeing to do. For example, I'll let you take ownership of my house if you pay me fill-in-the-blank amount of money. It's the same type of agreement we enter into when we buy a house or car, or legally promise to do anything.

That's what a covenant is too. As God's people, the Israelites promised to obey his commands (a covenant they broke, and it landed them in captivity). As God's modern-day people—his treasured possessions—we promise to have faith in Jesus's sacrifice and obey God's word with all our hearts. This isn't always an easy covenant to keep, but under this new agreement, God promises grace. How blessed are we?

DAY 158

"See what great love the Father has lavished on us, that we should be called children of God! And that is what we are! The reason the world does not know us is that it did not know him."

—1 JOHN 3:1

Being rejected by the world isn't easy. Most people look to their peers and loved ones for approval. Even if they're not pushed and pulled by the whims of what's trendy, a person may look to a specific group, like their circle of friends, for validation.

It's pretty much guaranteed you will be rejected by the world at some point—and probably many more times than once. Ouch. But even if (and when) the world turns against us, we can always rely on God to have our backs. His love isn't dependent on how the world responds to us.

And it's important we don't let the world's rejection stop us from sharing the gospel with others. We can't shy away from telling people about God's love. We can find refuge with our brothers and sisters in Christ—those who understand us and how our hearts have been touched by Jesus. But we can't stay locked in that safe space. If God's treasured possessions don't share his love with the world, who will?

DAY 159

"'On that day,' declares the Lord Almighty, 'I will take you, my servant Zerubbabel son of Shealtiel,' declares the Lord, 'and I will make you like my signet ring, for I have chosen you,' declares the Lord Almighty.'"

—HAGGAI 2:23

If you're not a history geek (yay!) or medieval fantasy nerd (guilty!), you might not be familiar with signet rings. Think of those big, bulky rings kings wear that have engravings on them. The engravings are usually a symbol of a particular family, like a crest, and the ring can be pressed into wax or clay, leaving behind the mark of that family or person. It's like a personal signature, and kings would often use them to seal declarations or letters to show the document's authenticity.

Now imagine God's signet ring. And imagine we're the clay, getting his personal signature pressed into us. God's treasured possessions are signed with his name. God's adored children are chosen and sealed with the Holy Spirit (Ephesians 4:30). This one is mine, his seal says. She belongs to me.

DAY 160

"Give thanks to the LORD, for he is good. His love endures forever."

—PSALM 136:1

No matter what happens to us in this world, God's love will never leave us. We belong to him in a real, lasting way. We belong to him forever! Are we surprised that he not only jealously protects his honor but protects his name *through* our lives—our words and actions, especially when we're representing him?

For those of us who have an independent nature, this idea might grate a little at first. I belong to him forever? No way! I'm my own person! Yes, you are, and God created you with all your wonderful unique characteristics. He loves you! But we also need to recognize his sovereignty over us. His eternal love is a gift, not a ball and chain.

DAY 161

"I am jealous for you with a godly jealousy. I promised you to one husband, to Christ, so that I might present you as a pure virgin to him."

—2 CORINTHIANS 11:2

God can be jealous without it being unwise or sinful. But can we? Is there such a thing as human holy jealousy? According to Paul in 2 Corinthians, yep, it's a thing.

For human beings who don't have God's perfectly good or sinless nature, holy jealousy happens when we're deeply committed to seeking the welfare or honor of someone. In this case, Paul felt that way about the Corinthian church he had started on one of his missionary journeys. He jealously sought to build them up, show them the right path, help them grow, lead them toward holiness. It was all for the welfare of the Corinthians and for God's glory.

And that's how we can know if the jealousy we feel is holy or not. Are we seeking honor or someone's welfare to build ourselves up? To enlarge our own egos? Or is it for the benefit of others and for God's glory? A solid heart-check should give us our answer. But holy jealousy *can* be a thing—a very good thing, in fact!

DAY 162

"They made him jealous with their foreign gods and angered him with their detestable idols."

—DEUTERONOMY 32:16

So what does God's jealousy look like? Many Old Testament verses that are connected to God's jealousy reference how he felt about the Israelites committing "spiritual adultery" with idols. He had made a covenant—a legal agreement—with them. They were to be his people and he was to be their God. He expected them to remain faithful to their promise to him. When they broke that promise and worshiped gods of wood and stone, God became jealous.

The same applies to us, even if we would never think of bowing down to a god of wood or stone. The point is that God insists on having first place in our lives and first place in our hearts. He can't and won't place second to our human relationships, our goals, or our hobbies. Those are all great things, but they aren't greater than God. Put God first and make him king of your life.

DAY 163

"Therefore prophesy concerning the land of Israel and say to the mountains and hills, to the ravines and valleys: 'This is what the Sovereign LORD says: I speak in my jealous wrath because you have suffered the scorn of the nations.'"

—EZEKIEL 36:6

Remember when we talked about how the world would reject us? How we could be rejected because of our faith? Even though the Bible tells us it will happen, God isn't okay with it. While he may not swoop in and save us from rejection, that doesn't mean God doesn't care when the world scorns us.

God is grieved by the persecution of his people. This verse from Ezekiel shows that even though the Israelites had repeatedly broken their covenant with God, God still felt jealous for his people when they suffered the scorn of other nations. When someone belittles or intentionally hurts you because you love Jesus, God sees that. He is jealous for you, for your honor, and for his honor. Even if we never feel vindicated on earth, it can comfort us to know that God isn't indifferent to that type of suffering.

DAY 164

"You desire but do not have, so you kill. You covet but you cannot get what you want, so you quarrel and fight. You do not have because you do not ask God. When you ask, you do not receive, because you ask with wrong motives, that you may spend what you get on your pleasures."

—JAMES 4:2–3

It may seem strange to have envy (covetousness) listed among the other nine commandments. I mean, jealousy and murder? Do they really belong on the same list?

But we see here that there's a connection between envy and other deeper sins. In fact, James says that "desiring but not having" (otherwise known as envy) is the root cause of some people quarreling, fighting, and even killing. Wow. So while envy is an internal sin we may be able to hide for a long while, it leaves us vulnerable to other "worse" sins—worse in the sense that it does damage to another person, not only ourselves.

Follow James's advice here. Search your heart. What are your reasons for wanting the things you don't have? Are they selfish reasons or honorable ones? If your reasons are honorable, ask God, in humility, for the things you desire. He is generous to his adored children when our hearts are clear of selfish desire.

DAY 165

"Then the angel who was speaking to me said, "Proclaim this word: This is what the LORD Almighty says: 'I am very jealous for Jerusalem and Zion.'"

—ZECHARIAH 1:14

It's not always easy to be part of God's family. We experience discipline, rebuke, correction, conviction, temptation to sin, struggle to resist temptation, and a host of other unpleasant, uncomfortable experiences at various points in our lives.

And that's because it hurts to be molded into something new. God is shaping us with all this loving correction—shaping us to look more and more like his Son.

This sometimes-painful shaping rises up from God's endless pool of love for us. He loves us too much to let us stay comfortable in our sin. He is "jealous" for us to belong to him, and him alone. When we're stuck in a cycle that is ultimately bad for us, as all bad choices and wrong attitudes are, God isn't content to leave us there. In the same way, it can hurt to deal with consequences from our parents, so it stings when our heavenly Father nudges us in the correct direction. But the growth we experience in Christlikeness and closeness to God is worth it!

DAY 166

"Ephraim, what more have I to do with idols? I will answer him and care for him. I am like a flourishing juniper; your fruitfulness comes from me."

—HOSEA 14:8

We could probably come up with a dozen reasons why idolatry is so offensive to God and stokes his jealousy like nothing else. One of those reasons is that, when we put other things before God in our lives and hearts, we fail to acknowledge him as our source.

Everything we have has been placed in our lives by God. Yes, even the things you worked really, really hard for—those things came from God. God wants us to be hard workers. But having the opportunity to work hard or the ability to excel isn't something we can create out of thin air. God has placed us in the position to do so, or blessed us with particular gifts that allow us to excel.

When we acknowledge God as the source of everything good, we bring honor to him and guard against idols in our lives.

DAY 167

"Those who cling to worthless idols turn away from God's love for them."

—JONAH 2:8

Idolatry doesn't just offend God. It actually hurts us too. When we turn toward something else—whether it's another person, a thing, or even ourselves—and we give that "something else" first place in our hearts, we are turning away from God's love.

Yikes. It's a scary thought. Why would we want to turn away from the vast love of the God of the universe? Well, we've covered several reasons why we can be tempted to turn away from God's love. It's not always easy to be one of God's treasured possessions. It wasn't easy for the Israelites, and it's not easy for us. Having faith forces us to change.

But the rewards for continuing to seek hard after God and turning away from the things that would tempt us are beyond measure. The peace, joy, love, endurance, compassion, and righteousness that result from an ongoing relationship with Jesus are worth the hard work. Embrace God's great love; don't turn away from it.

DAY 168

"I have been crucified with Christ and I no longer live, but Christ lives in me. The life I now live in the body, I live by faith in the Son of God, who loved me and gave himself for me."

—GALATIANS 2:20

It's a pretty amazing thing to have God's Holy Spirit living inside us. The Spirit is our seal, God's family stamp on us. But the Spirit is also our helper and our guide, encouraging and enabling us toward lives of holiness—lives that don't poke at God's jealousy.

How can we know if we're following the Spirit? The Holy Spirit will always push us toward God's will and his Word. So if you're feeling pushed or pulled to do something God's Word forbids, that's not the Holy Spirit talking to you. It's most likely an outside force like peer pressure, or it's an "inside force," meaning our own natural bent to do what we want without examining it against God's Word.

The leading of the Holy Spirit is a great gift and will propel us toward lives of holiness, humility, and love.

DAY 169

"A heart at peace gives life to the body, but envy rots the bones."

—PROVERBS 14:30

In English, jealousy and envy are synonyms. And there definitely are parallels between the two words. But there are a few differences, too, that should help us understand why envy is never okay and jealousy sometimes is (when it's holy jealousy).

Biblical holy jealousy is about guarding and protecting—protecting honor or welfare. Envy and sinful jealousy are about covetousness, which means wanting something someone else has. Envy is rooted in discontent with what we have or who we are. It looks at our lot in life, looks at someone else's lot in life, and says, "I'm not satisfied with what I have. I want what she has." Resentment builds. Thankfulness evaporates. Even darker sins are born from the resentment. Envy eats at us from the inside out.

How do we guard against envy? By practicing peace and contentment. When you're tempted to covet, think instead about all the ways *you* have been blessed, all the mercies God has shown to you. Thank him for those things. By focusing on what we do have, we practice thankfulness and guard against sinful jealousy.

DAY 170

"The acts of the flesh are obvious: sexual immorality, impurity and debauchery; idolatry and witchcraft; hatred, discord, jealousy, fits of rage, selfish ambition, dissensions, factions . . ."

—GALATIANS 5:19–20

It's easy to think of jealousy as no big deal. It's not usually something others can see; it's something we feel. So it's possible that you could walk through your entire life with jealousy gnawing at your peace, and people may never know.

But when we look at Paul's letter to the Galatians, we see that he has listed jealousy among some pretty nasty sins. Jealousy is sandwiched between hatred, discord, and fits of rage. Yikes. Sounds like a pretty big deal. Like hatred, jealousy is the type of internal struggle that denies some basic truths about God. That makes it very dangerous.

What are those truths? God is in control. He has blessed each of us in the best way possible for our situation. God is a generous God. We aren't in a position to tell him he hasn't done enough. Don't let comparison steal your joy! Thank God for all he's done for you.

DAY 171

"For where you have envy and selfish ambition, there you find disorder and every evil practice."

—JAMES 3:16

James puts envy and selfish ambition right next to each other in the third chapter of his letter. Why? Because both envy and selfish ambition are rooted in self-importance. Wait a minute. I thought self-esteem was a good thing! It is, to a point.

What's the difference between self-importance and self-esteem? Self-esteem, when in balance, acknowledges that we are loved by God. We are his beautiful, beloved daughters. We don't need to listen to a world that tells us we should look or be a certain way. Balanced self-esteem tells us to embrace God's view of us, and that's a great thing.

Self-importance seeks to put us in the place of God—to make us the ones deserving of honor and praise. To acknowledge ourselves, not God, as our source of good things. Self-importance makes an idol out of *me*. Remember God as the source of all goodness—your identity, your relationship with Jesus, and all the blessings you have in this life—and you will keep from falling into the trap of self-importance.

DAY 172

"Anger is cruel and fury overwhelming, but who can stand before jealousy?"

—PROVERBS 27:4

Sometimes, you just don't click with a person. You may be able to have a decent, civil relationship, but you and that person will never be best friends. Other times, a person can really rub you the wrong way and you have to actively fight against annoyance—and even anger—whenever you interact with them.

And then there are people who are your friends. The ones you click with and genuinely enjoy, and you're pretty sure will be your besties for life. Those are the relationships you should most actively guard against jealousy. What?!

Yep. Jealousy isn't like anger or fury or hatred. When we feel fury or hatred, they're obvious—they can even overwhelm us. But jealousy is a sneaky sin. It invades close relationships. It starts small, with a seed of envy. If it's not uprooted quickly, it grows into a vine that chokes even the healthiest of friendships. Beware of letting seeds of envy destroy your most precious friendships.

DAY 173

"But in your hearts revere Christ as Lord. Always be prepared to give an answer to everyone who asks you to give the reason for the hope that you have. But do this with gentleness and respect."

—1 PETER 3:15

If God's jealousy means that he continually seeks to protect his own honor, how can we, as his daughters, reflect that trait and protect God's honor too?

It can be a supremely awkward moment when you're hanging out with people who do something that dishonors God. What do you say? How do you react? Do you preach a sermon on the spot? Stomp away in a huff and refuse to listen to another word? Keep your mouth shut and hope it's over soon?

While these moments are awkward, and sometimes painful, we can view them as ministry opportunities. Peter says to always be prepared to give an answer. That doesn't mean a snarky comeback. It means a declaration of God's grace and love in our lives. That applies to those moments when people are actively dishonoring God with their words or actions. And, while we may feel passionately defensive for God, Peter says to answer with gentleness and respect. Doing so gives us a much better chance of being heard than responding indignantly with anger.

DAY 174

"Do not let any unwholesome talk come out of your mouths, but only what is helpful for building others up according to their needs, that it may benefit those who listen."

—EPHESIANS 4:29

Ready for a tough truth? Oftentimes when people are dishonoring God or raising objections to him, it's actually God's followers they're objecting to—our hypocrisy or lack of love. Ouch. That truth hurts because we want to represent Jesus well to the world, not detract from his goodness with our failures. The truth hurts even more because we know there are people out there who call themselves Christians but don't act like Christ.

While we're never going to be perfect, it's important that we seek to show true faith to the world. Paul's word to the Ephesians here are a great start. Guarding what comes out of our mouths—or fingertips on the Internet—is essential. We want to build others up, not tear them down. We want to demonstrate love, not anger or meanness or disdain. Love others with your words and your actions, and you'll be protecting God's honor.

DAY 175

"But if you harbor bitter envy and selfish ambition in your hearts, do not boast about it or deny the truth."

—JAMES 3:14

Sins harbored in our hearts are destructive and cancerous. They eat us up and rob us of so many good things God wants us to have in our hearts. But the sin becomes compounded even further when it spills from our hearts out of our mouths.

Why? Because then, not only are we allowing ourselves to be swallowed by our sins, we're doing damage to God's honor among the world. This is the opposite of what his holy jealousy seeks to accomplish.

Heart-check time. Do you have envy and selfish ambition in your heart right now? Is there something someone else has that you've been jealously wanting for yourself? Ask God to help you rid the selfish desire from your life. Ask him to help you better represent him to the world. The desire to present a better witness to the world for God's sake is a holy one. God will answer those prayers!

"Let the message of Christ dwell among you richly as you teach and admonish one another with all wisdom through psalms, hymns, and songs from the Spirit, singing to God with gratitude in your hearts."

—COLOSSIANS 3:16

Christianity is a religion that befuddles the world. At its core, it's different than all others because being a Christian is not about what you do, who you are, or what you're born into. There isn't a list of things one must do in order to earn salvation. The Christian's salvation comes from Christ alone—it's about what *he* did on the cross, not what we do for ourselves. Period.

But . . . is that all? Is there more to the story? This is an area where Christians get tripped up. Either we fall into the trap of mistakenly believing our good works somehow save us or make us worthy of God's love. Or we go too far in the other direction and fail to grow in our faith after receiving our salvation. These Christians live lives just as worldly as their unsaved neighbors. Is that really what God wants from his children?

We must continually acknowledge Jesus as the source of our salvation. But we must also seek to live lives worthy of the grace we've already received. It's not to earn that grace, which is impossible. It's to bring honor to God's name and continue spreading and enriching his kingdom.

DAY 177

"Now this is what the LORD Almighty says: 'Give careful thought to your ways.'"

—HAGGAI 1:5

Want a practical way to bring honor to God? Focus on thoughtfulness. We live in an increasingly thoughtless world—a world that only wants to be entertained and can only think in meme-length and meme-depth.

Challenge yourself to be a thoughtful follower of Jesus instead. That means being quick to listen and slow to speak. That means putting others first and making efforts to reach out, crossing boundaries to show love to those who are different from us. It means working the spots of meanness, carelessness, and selfishness out of our hearts.

Think of one way you can move away from carelessness toward thoughtfulness. Pray about it. Ask God to help you in that area and keep it at the forefront of your mind as you move through your day. Do you notice a change in how you feel and how others respond to you? Enjoy that! Let it propel you toward greater and greater thoughtfulness. That brings honor to our Lord.

DAY 178

"Whom have I in heaven but you? And earth has nothing I desire besides you."

—PSALM 73:25

There are a lot of beautiful things on earth. God's intricate creations found in nature would take more than a lifetime to study and fully appreciate. God made mankind like him, capable of creativity, kindness, holiness, generosity, and goodness. He gave us relationships with parents, friends, siblings, spouses, and others for our joy. We have food to enjoy, air to breathe, and life to live.

And still, the psalmist says that earth has nothing he desires more than God. That's because, as beautiful and wonderful as this earth is, it pales in comparison to God's great beauty. God is the ultimate expression of all desirable qualities—all good things are found in him, and to the highest degree. Wow!

Those wonderful things we love about our lives on earth are each reflections of some aspect of God. These reflections give us glimpses of our Father whose beauty is complete.

DAY 179

"Because of the LORD's great love we are not consumed, for his compassions never fail. They are new every morning; great is your faithfulness."

—LAMENTATIONS 3:22–23

God's desirable qualities are boundless. There probably isn't enough paper in the world to list and examine them all. But the Bible gives us plenty of them to think about! Just in this passage alone, the prophet Jeremiah lists three awesome ones: God's great love, his never-failing compassions, and his faithfulness.

Take a few moments right now to think and pray about that. God's love for you is indescribably huge. His compassion for you, his adored daughter, will never fail. And he is perfectly faithful—never going back on his word, never neglecting a promise, never ceasing to be who he is.

In thankfulness for God's good qualities, think of ways you can spread his love to others. Do you know someone who needs God's message of grace right now? We all probably do. Share the good news of your great God with someone today!

"Whoever does not love does not know God, because God is love."

—1 JOHN 4:8

There are lots of different things the Bible teaches us that are important. It's important to understand God's holiness. It's important to understand God's moral law and how Jesus wants us to live our lives as his followers. It's important to stand firm on the truths and promises of the Bible.

But the single most important thing the Word of God teaches us about is love. When Jesus was asked which commandment was most important, he summed up the entire law by saying we must love God and love our neighbors (Mark 12:29). Here, the apostle John says God *is* love—pure, perfect love—and if we don't love others, then we don't know God.

If you've failed at this, don't worry. It doesn't mean your relationship with God isn't real. We all fail. John's point isn't to make you doubt the realness of your faith. His point is to show us, without question, the most important of God's desirable qualities we must reflect—his love.

DAY 181

"How great you are, Sovereign LORD! There is no one like you, and there is no God but you, as we have heard with our own ears."

—2 SAMUEL 7:22

God truly is unparalleled. There's no one like him. Nothing in the universe rivals his beauty. But the Bible does give us some cool metaphors to help us get a mental picture of what God is like. And each metaphor gives us a different view of his amazing qualities.

The Bible calls God our shepherd, and we're his sheep—being led, cared for, and protected by his watchful eye (Psalm 23:1). Several verses compare God the Father and Jesus to a rock—strong, unshakable, dependable (Psalm 18:2). Isaiah says God is the potter and we are the clay (Isaiah 64:8). We're the work of his hands, and he's constantly shaping and molding us. God is a spring of living water, refreshing and restoring us (Jeremiah 17:13). God is a consuming fire—powerful and untamed (Deuteronomy 4:24).

By looking at some of these poetic descriptions of God, we see many of his remarkable traits. See how many word-pictures you can find about God as you read the Bible. What does each of them tell you about the God who loves you beyond measure?

DAY 182

"From Zion, perfect in beauty, God shines forth."

—PSALM 50:2

God's beauty and perfection go hand-in-hand. God is beautiful in that he is the sum of all desirable qualities, and he is perfect in that he lacks no part of any desirable quality. For God, "perfect" is a great thing!

But what about us? Perfectionism is a struggle for many people. We long to achieve—to be the best at what we do—and it can be soul-crushing to fail, which we inevitably do sometimes. For the perfectionist, if the failure doesn't crush her, it propels her toward greater and greater perfectionism, always seeking the thrill of the next A+. It's an unhealthy cycle that pushes us toward the false belief that our worth lies in our achievement.

So what's a perfectionist to do? It's okay to do well. In fact, doing well at the tasks we undertake can reflect God. But a healthy focus is to strive for God-glorifying excellence, rather than perfection, and to remember to give ourselves grace if—and when—we fail.

DAY 183

"If you love those who love you, what reward will you get? Are not even the tax collectors doing that? And if you greet only your own people, what are you doing more than others? Do not even pagans do that? Be perfect, therefore, as your heavenly Father is perfect."

—MATTHEW 5:46–48

Jesus has some strong words for us here. Again he's speaking about love, the most important trait of God we can possibly reflect. And he tells us we are not only to love our "own people" (which would mean those you're close to, like family members and friends, as well as those to whom you relate because of culture, shared heritage, shared interests, or shared faith), but our love should cross all of those boundaries, otherwise we're doing no better than the pagans and tax collectors of Jesus's day.

And it's within that context that Jesus tells us to be "perfect." The Greek word there is *telios* and it means *brought to its end*—completed and whole. So Jesus is telling us to let our love for others be boundless, like the Father's. He's telling us to show complete, whole, perfect love. Think about what that means for your life. Are there ways you can show wider, deeper love for those who may not be "your people" but whom God loves dearly?

DAY 184

"But the Lord *said to Samuel, 'Do not consider his appearance or his height, for I have rejected him. The* Lord *does not look at the things people look at. People look at the outward appearance, but the* Lord *looks at the heart.'"*

—1 SAMUEL 16:7

When we say the word "beauty," we usually think of outward appearance. Our culture is obsessed with it. Cosmetics companies sell many *billions* of dollars' worth of products every single year. It's safe to say that many women are at least a little insecure about the way they look. With the amount of pressure our culture places on girls and women to look a certain way, it's no wonder.

The Bible acknowledges that outer beauty is a thing. Some of the women mentioned in the Bible are specifically said to have had outward beauty (Sarah, Rebecca, Rachel, and Esther, to name a few). But, while outward beauty is mentioned, the Bible often affirms the idea that outward appearances don't matter to God. God looks at the heart, not what sort of package that heart is wrapped in.

When we feel insecure about the way we look, we can ask God to help us focus on the important things. A woman who is humble before God and confident of her Lord's love is always beautiful!

DAY 185

"Leah had weak eyes, but Rachel had a lovely figure and was beautiful."

—GENESIS 29:17

Comparison is tough to handle, especially among siblings and close friends. In this verse, we have two sisters being compared—and these two sisters went on to share the same husband. Yikes.

Have you ever felt like the "weak-eyed" sister? In English, we tend to read this verse as though Leah had bad eyesight or that her "weak eyes" were another way of saying she wasn't pretty, given that the second part of the verse is talking about how beautiful her sister was.

But the Hebrew word for *weak* means *tender* or *gentle*. While Jacob fell in love immediately with the beauty queen sister, Rachel, the Hebrew phrase for "weak eyes" has suggestions of virtue and God's favor. God consistently saw that Leah was not as loved as Rachel, and he blessed her, making her the mother of six of Jacob's sons. It is through Leah's line that Jesus's heritage is traced (via Judah) and Leah's son Levi was the father of the priestly tribe of Israel. God blessed Leah greatly! If you feel like you're being compared, especially based on your outward appearance, remember what truly matters to God.

DAY 186

"There Abraham and his wife Sarah were buried, there Isaac and his wife Rebekah were buried, and there I buried Leah."

—GENESIS 49:31

Jacob always favored Rachel, even though Leah was the mother of six of his sons. Rachel eventually gave Jacob two sons, Joseph and Benjamin, and unsurprisingly, those sons were Jacob's favorites. This favoritism had long been a problem in Jacob's family, and even led to his other sons committing a horrible crime against Joseph and selling him into slavery in Egypt. That's some next-level sibling rivalry! Thankfully God brought about good through Joseph, and the family was eventually reconciled.

But here, as Jacob is about to die, he says something interesting that perhaps raises more questions than it answers. After the rivalry between Rachel and Leah, after how heavily Jacob favored Rachel and her sons, he chose to bury Leah in the family tomb with his grandparents and parents, where he himself asked to be buried. Could it be that, at the end of his days, Jacob finally saw what God saw in Leah? Did he finally learn that Leah, though perhaps not as beautiful as Rachel, had been a good wife to him?

The Bible doesn't say for sure. But it does say that God remembered and blessed Leah because he looks past outward appearances.

DAY 187

"I praise you because I am fearfully and wonderfully made; your works are wonderful, I know that full well."

—PSALM 139:14

Outward beauty is a funny thing. It can seem like something set in stone—either I'm pretty or I'm not, and there's nothing I can do about it. But in truth, what cultures define as "beautiful" changes drastically. Every body type you can imagine has been considered ideal at some point in history. Certain facial features that might be airbrushed away these days were considered the standard of aristocratic beauty a few hundred years ago in Europe.

Culture shifts. God doesn't. And God says that, no matter what our current society's standard of outward appearance is, you *are* beautiful. You are fearfully and wonderfully made. God crafted you with love. He made each of us a little masterpiece, a wondrous combination of our parents' genetic traits—unique and full of all the tiny miracles of life. This is true of each of us. We bear the thumbprint of God.

DAY 188

"Rather, it should be that of your inner self, the unfading beauty of a gentle and quiet spirit, which is of great worth in God's sight."

—1 PETER 3:4

Outer beauty fades. Our looks are transient in nature, meaning we change as we age. When we're young, it may not seem very important to recognize that truth and understand God's view of fading outer beauty. But when you live in a culture that reveres youth, it's never too soon to grab hold of this idea.

Our inner selves are where true beauty is found. And Peter says true beauty is a gentle and quiet spirit. It's quite a contrast to the brash, flashy focus on outward appearance we're used to. Humble, gentle, and quiet of spirit, Peter says. Those things don't fade as we age; they get better. If we spend our lives growing and maturing in Jesus, becoming more and more like God's Son, then our peaceful, gracious spirit only gets better with time.

There's nothing wrong with taking care of our appearances or wanting to be clean and put-together. There's nothing wrong with enjoying fashion. But we should recognize the transient nature of these things. The soul is what sticks around, so let's make sure we care *most* about nurturing that.

DAY 189

"Do not neglect your gift, which was given you through prophecy when the body of elders laid their hands on you."

—1 TIMOTHY 4:14

It doesn't matter if you feel like an awkward wallflower, if you are fairly comfortable in your own skin, or if you were born with the features and confidence of a supermodel. No matter what you look like, your looks are not the best thing you have to offer the world. By far.

How can I say that without even knowing you? Because the Bible so frequently affirms our outside appearance is irrelevant. What you look like has no bearing on your worth in God's eyes. He has gifted each of us with talents, passions, and godly characteristics, whether it's a supernatural reliance on God, an ability to understand Scripture in depth, a great gift for hospitality, an extra-kind heart, or some other spiritual gift that reflects God's nature.

These are the best things about us. Our souls and spirits, not the outward appearance, which fades. Thank God for the awesome soul he gave to you. There's a reason—many, in fact—that he loves you so much!

DAY 190

"You are altogether beautiful, my darling; there is no flaw in you."

—SONG OF SONGS 4:7

Have you ever gotten so caught up in your insecurities about your looks or your body that you can't imagine anyone will ever find you attractive? If so, you're not alone. A lot of girls and women have this sort of body-image struggle. It can lead to depression, eating disorders, and other mental health problems. If you find you're in need of mental health help, reach out to someone you trust! You don't need to feel alone.

And we also need to reject the idea that no one could ever be attracted to us. Godly men see their mates the way the writer of Song of Songs saw his beloved. Altogether beautiful. Darling. Loved. Flawless. Adored.

If being married is a desire God has put in your heart for the future, start praying for your spouse. When you date potential mates, pray for discernment and wisdom. A man who adores you doesn't nitpick supposed "flaws" the way you might when you stand before the mirror. And while we're at it, stop doing that! You're beautiful!

DAY 191

"I also want the women to dress modestly, with decency and propriety, adorning themselves, not with elaborate hairstyles or gold or pearls or expensive clothes, but with good deeds, appropriate for women who profess to worship God."

—1 TIMOTHY 2:9–10

Modesty matters—at least according to Paul. And it's usually wise to listen to him. In recent years, modesty has been getting a lot of airtime in the online Christian community. Everyone has a different opinion of where the modesty line is drawn, so how are we supposed to know what's okay and what's not?

More than the amount of skin being shown, Paul focuses on the women in church dressing simply and not wearing their wealth, so to speak. And yes, he says to be decent, which also applies to the amount of skin showing. We should never feel pressured to show skin, wear expensive clothes, pile on the jewelry, or otherwise draw attention to our outward appearances. Once again, we see that the things that matter most are not related to how we look. Paul says he wants the women of Timothy's church to be clothed with good deeds. Wrap yourself in good deeds today! (But probably put on some clothes too.)

DAY 192

"A wife of noble character who can find? She is worth far more than rubies."

—PROVERBS 31:10

Proverbs gives us a really cool picture of what makes a woman beautiful in God's sight. The "wife of noble character" passage in Proverbs 31 is famous for a reason. We see through these passages that this noble woman is not a "trophy wife," existing as an adornment to her husband—a doll to be paraded as his prized possession (yuck). And she's also not one step up from a slave, the way women were, and still are, in some cultures. The Proverbs 31 woman avoids both of these female stereotypes.

She is honored and revered—the manager of the household and the one who keeps matters moving for her husband and children. But we shouldn't mistakenly believe this portrait of a noble woman can only apply to a woman who is married or has children. All of us can benefit from examining God's Word carefully here to uncover the ultimate portrait of a beautiful woman the way God sees her.

DAY 193

"She brings him good, not harm, all the days of her life."

—PROVERBS 31:12

A woman of godly beauty brings good to others and avoids causing harm. Goodness means mercy, grace, and patience. A beautiful woman pours those things into the lives of those around her. She has compassion and is slow to anger. She cares about those who are in distress. She is sensitive to the needs of others.

And she actively avoids doing harm. Most of the time, we do harm without meaning to. Most followers of Jesus aren't searching for ways to hurt other people. And yet we manage to do so sometimes. So how do we avoid it? Practicing thoughtfulness is a great way rein in hasty words and actions that can hurt others. We should also seek to follow Jesus's command, the so-called Golden Rule found in Matthew 7:12: Do unto others as you would have them do unto you.

DAY 194

"She selects wool and flax and works with eager hands. She is like the merchant ships, bringing her food from afar. She gets up while it is still night; she provides food for her family and portions for her female servants."

—PROVERBS 31:13–15

A woman of godly beauty is industrious. Back in biblical times, this looked a little different than it does for most of us now. In Bible days, the female head of household, along with her daughters or female servants, would be providing clothing and food for the household. Can we just take a moment to be thankful we aren't responsible for spinning our own wool?

But being industrious is still a great quality. So what does that mean for us? It can mean anything from baking to building robots, from gardening to writing music. Basically, if you're making, building, doing, creating, or working, you're doing it right. When we make things, we reflect our wildly creative God. Sticking with a particular craft, hobby, or discipline over a period of time also builds skill, which helps us reflect God with excellence. And, to be fair, so does spinning wool, so feel free to give that a shot too, if you want.

DAY 195

"She considers a field and buys it; out of her earnings she plants a vineyard. She sees that her trading is profitable, and her lamp does not go out at night."

—PROVERBS 31:16, 18

A woman of godly beauty is a smart businesswoman. Yep, you read that right. Even in the vastly different culture of the Old Testament where a woman's work most frequently centered on the home, we have this fascinating part of the passage.

This doesn't mean you have to be a business owner in order to be woman of godly beauty. But it does mean we should be wise with our finances and shrewd with our business dealings. We should be thrifty, not wasteful. We should do our research before making big purchases and enlist the help of experts, when necessary. And if you're drawn to the business world as a career, hold yourself to the highest standard of business ethics.

Whether we're spending the majority of our time caring for a household, working in an office, or balancing some combination of the two, we can be the Proverbs 31 smart businesswoman.

DAY 196

"She opens her arms to the poor and extends her hands to the needy."

—PROVERBS 31:20

A woman of godly beauty is generous with her time and love. And she's not just generous to her friends or family. It doesn't cost us much to show love and generosity to the people closest to us.

We're meant to share with the people who need it most. The homeless community. Women and children in domestic abuse shelters. Kids whose parents aren't around much, kids who need a good role model or a friend.

There are so many people, even in our own cities and towns, who would qualify as poor and needy in some way. And the woman of godly beauty is generous to these people. She helps them with open arms. Think of ways you can care for those who need help in your community.

DAY 197

"When it snows, she has no fear for her household; for all of them are clothed in scarlet."

—PROVERBS 31:21

Don't worry. This verse doesn't mean you always have to clothe yourself—or anyone else, for that matter—in red. If you like red, go ahead and rock that scarlet, but that's not really the point of the verse. What this verse is talking about is prosperity and planning. A woman of godly beauty thinks ahead.

Even though we know God is working his will in each of our lives and he is the one who determines our steps, the Bible encourages us to plan ahead with wisdom. We are to make good use of our time and resources, faithfully managing whatever God puts into our hands, whether a little or a lot.

Are there areas in your life that would be improved by better planning—schoolwork, chores, your social calendar, or even your bigger plans for the future? Take some time to thoughtfully consider your next steps.

"She is clothed with strength and dignity; she can laugh at the days to come."

—PROVERBS 31:25

A woman of godly beauty possesses inner strength. Again we look to the inner self instead the outward appearance to find true beauty. Strength and dignity are our clothing. The godly woman carries herself well, and because of her godly wisdom, she can laugh at the future. In other words, she has no reason to fear the future.

Fear can be a powerful—and powerfully unhealthy—motivator. Unless we're talking about the holy "fear of the Lord," fear can cause us to make some pretty bad decisions. Decisions that put ourselves above others or cause us to shy away from our faith. Instead, when we're clothed from the inside out with strength and dignity, we have no reason to fear. God is with us. Our foundation is secure. We can face tomorrow with laughter and look forward to the distant day when God says to us, "Well done, good and faithful servant" (Matthew 25:23).

DAY 199

"She speaks with wisdom, and faithful instruction is on her tongue."

—PROVERBS 31:26

A woman of godly beauty is filled with wisdom. This doesn't mean we need to spend all of our time focused on serious, somber things. It's okay to have fun and indulge in a little silliness. But godly women should give thought to important matters so we can speak with wisdom on such things.

And we shouldn't stop at possessing or speaking with wisdom. We should intentionally seek to give faithful instruction to others. This can mean anything from teaching younger siblings to being a mentor to someone, or giving a friend good advice. The point is to be a wise voice of godly instruction for others. If we don't, voices that *aren't* rooted in godly wisdom will speak out on important matters instead.

"She watches over the affairs of her household and does not eat the bread of idleness."

—PROVERBS 31:27

How does a day of comfort-TV binge-watching sound? Or maybe you'd rather be snuggled under the covers reading books and sipping something warm and delicious. Or maybe you'd like to lounge on a beach somewhere, enjoying the sun, sand, and surf. All of those sound like fantastic ways to spend a day. And they are!

We all need rest and recuperation sometimes. The biblical principle of the Sabbath shows us that rest matters to God, so we shouldn't feel guilty about taking breaks or enjoying relaxation. But these are moments of rest—pauses in the daily rhythm of life. And in our daily rhythm of life, we see that a woman of godly beauty isn't lazy. Rest is good—required, even. But on the whole, we should strive to avoid idleness and be productive and efficient in whatever we set our hands to.

DAY 201

"Her children arise and call her blessed; her husband also, and he praises her."

—PROVERBS 31:28

Do we *have* to be married and have kids in order to be a woman of godly beauty? The answer is, of course, a resounding *no.* The apostle Paul even writes in the New Testament that some people are gifted with singleness and no desire to marry so that they can focus solely on ministry (1 Corinthians 7:34). Even if you'd like to be married at some point in the future, Paul's words show us that we don't need to be married in order to be serving God well and fully.

What this verse really means is that others speak well of a woman of godly beauty. In other words, she has a good reputation. She is wise, generous, and compassionate. She lives out those qualities in her life, and others take notice. They think well of her and they say so. Let's be the kind of women others can't help but say good things about.

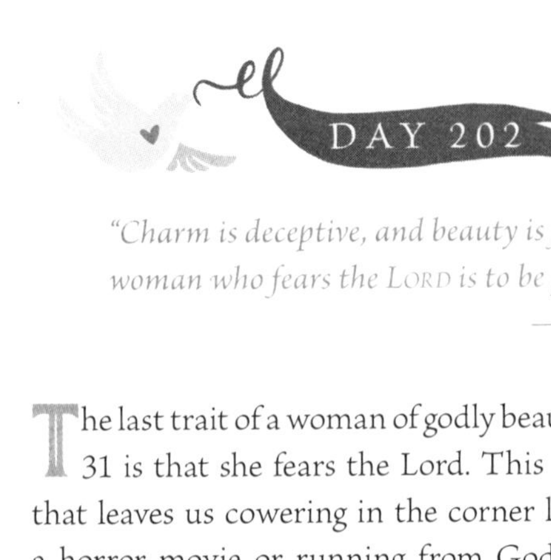

DAY 202

"Charm is deceptive, and beauty is fleeting; but a woman who fears the Lord is to be praised."

—PROVERBS 31:30

The last trait of a woman of godly beauty listed in Proverbs 31 is that she fears the Lord. This isn't the sort of fear that leaves us cowering in the corner like we're trapped in a horror movie or running from God like he's some sort of monster. This type of fear means honor and respect. A woman of godly beauty has such deep, profound respect for the Lord, it motivates and inspires everything she does. He is the foundation of her life. His Word is the source of her wisdom.

This verse contrasts honor and respect for God with charm and outward beauty. A person with charisma may or may not have any real substance. And even magazine-cover beauty fades with time. But respect for God lasts forever. It infuses every part of our earthly life and follows us into eternity.

DAY 203

"There is no fear in love. But perfect love drives out fear, because fear has to do with punishment. The one who fears is not made perfect in love."

—1 JOHN 4:18

Love is the most beautiful thing in the world. God's love is the source of all the good things he gives to us—our free offer of salvation, the Holy Spirit to guide us, spiritual gifts, material provision. All of those things, and a great many others, flow from God's love for us.

Sometimes we struggle to understand God's love because it doesn't look quite like ours. When we say "love," we tend to think of a feeling. Emotional love. But God's love isn't like that. It isn't based on how he feels or how we feel. It's based on who he is. He loves us because he says so, and he doesn't go back on his word.

We can learn to love like God. It doesn't come naturally all the time, but by continually putting others before ourselves, we begin to build a godly, selfless love—one not swayed by feelings that may flash intensely for a moment, then fade. That type of love is unwavering, lasting, and beautiful.

DAY 204

"Your beauty should not come from outward adornment, such as elaborate hairstyles and the wearing of gold jewelry or fine clothes."

—1 PETER 3:3

With all this talk against outward adornment—including comments on hairstyles, of all things—how do we know where to draw the line? Are we required to wear no makeup and plain clothes all the time? Without comments specific to our culture, how do we know when we've gone too far in God's eyes?

It's really a matter of priorities. Is your choice of clothing so important to you that you would spend all of your money on a new outfit without using any of it to tithe? Are you so concerned with your hair looking perfect that you would never serve on a mission field, whether at home or abroad, because you'd be embarrassed about not having access to your curling iron? Is it the worst thing you can possibly imagine to be seen without makeup on? Questions like these can help reveal our hearts. If vanity has become a real priority—or especially a top priority—we've gone too far.

DAY 205

"He has made everything beautiful in its time. He has also set eternity in the human heart; yet no one can fathom what God has done from beginning to end."

—ECCLESIASTES 3:11

Life is full of seasons. Some are related to our age—childhood, adolescence, adulthood, the golden years. Others are related to our work of the moment—high school, college, career, retirement. And others are marked by our relationships—dating, marriage, parenthood, caring for elderly parents, *being* the elderly parents.

Sometimes we have seasons that are characterized by their level of difficulty—a joy-filled season, or one that pushes us to our absolute limit. When we're slogging through a difficult time, it can be hard to appreciate that season. But the Bible says God has made everything beautiful in its time. Each season, whether joyous or trying, is filled with God's beauty. And we can always find the beauty if we're willing to look.

Sometimes that beauty is seen in tiny pinpricks of light shining through the darkness—itty-bitty love letters from God that let us know, hey, life is tough but you're not alone. Other times, the difficulty itself *is* the beauty, refining us through fire, shaping us into who God wants us to be. Embrace life's seasons. Find the beauty.

DAY 206

"Jesus answered, 'If you want to be perfect, go, sell your possessions and give to the poor, and you will have treasure in heaven. Then come, follow me.'"

—MATTHEW 19:21

If you live in a prosperous society, reading this verse can feel like swallowing a very large, difficult pill. Do we have to sell everything to obey Jesus's words? Do we have to give our entire paychecks to the poor to be true followers?

Don't panic. This was a specific directive to a specific man. Jesus didn't command all his followers to do this. But Jesus singled out this man for an important reason, and we would all do well to pay attention. It wasn't simply because he was rich or prosperous. It was because he valued his wealth so deeply, it was a hindrance to his faith. How do we know? Because of how the man reacted to Jesus's words. He went away sad and didn't obey the command. The price of following Jesus was too high. He had put his faith in his wealth and wasn't willing to part with it.

The question isn't "*Must* we sell all our possessions?" but rather "*Could* we sell all our possessions?" Would we, if Jesus asked us to? Make sure you're not putting your hope in material wealth. Let your trust in God alone inspire wild, radical generosity toward others.

DAY 207

"The kingdom of heaven is like treasure hidden in a field. When a man found it, he hid it again, and then in his joy went and sold all he had and bought that field."

—MATTHEW 13:44

Money has always been a bit of a sticking point for mankind, it seems. Even back in Jesus's time, he used material wealth as an example to drive home the point of just how precious the kingdom of God is.

In Jesus's parable, the man sold everything he had to buy a field in which a precious treasure was buried—and Jesus said that precious treasure is God's kingdom. Material wealth and the comfort, security, and safety it provides often feels incredibly important to us. And it's not entirely unimportant—we certainly need material items such as food, shelter, and clothing to survive. But Jesus drives home the point that the kingdom of heaven is worth far more than any of these things. Your salvation is more precious and costlier than anything you could ever own.

How highly prioritized is your relationship with God in your life? Is it the most important thing, or is it all the way down the list somewhere? Think about how deeply your worldview, your attitude, and your actions would be affected if God's kingdom shot to the top of your priority list.

DAY 208

"Besides, in my devotion to the temple of my God I now give my personal treasures of gold and silver for the temple of my God, over and above everything I have provided for this holy temple."

—1 CHRONICLES 29:3

Personal generosity matters. Giving freely of your money, time, and talents is one of the most effective ways to show people the love of Christ without preaching at them. When people who have not heard the Gospel see others who sacrifice time to volunteer or who give money to help those in need or who use their gifts in ways that help others instead of themselves, they have to stop and ask themselves *why*.

And in a me-focused society, people do stop and take notice. And when we're asked what drives our generosity, the answer is simple: We give to honor the God who has given to us. We give to show tangible love to our neighbors, just as Jesus instructed us to.

What personal treasures can you give today?

DAY 209

"Do not store up for yourselves treasures on earth, where moths and vermin destroy, and where thieves break in and steal. But store up for yourselves treasures in heaven, where moths and vermin do not destroy, and where thieves do not break in and steal."

—MATTHEW 6:19–20

Earthly treasures come in many shapes and sizes. We tend to think only of money, and that is one example, but there are other kinds of earthly treasures. A successful career, a big house, worldly achievements, or even the perfect family. It's not wrong to work hard at your career, own a nice home, or strive for excellence, and it's certainly not wrong to pour time and energy into your family.

But all of these pursuits are passing. Even men and women who were mighty in their time are, eventually, reduced to a few lines in a history book. Everything about this life is temporary. But heavenly treasure is eternal. Saved souls are saved for eternity. Heavenly rewards for kindness shown in Christian love or persecution endured for Jesus's name or participating in the growth of the kingdom of God will last forever.

Think of ways to increase your heavenly "bank account" while putting less emphasis on worldly riches.

DAY 210

"Cornelius stared at him in fear. 'What is it, Lord?' he asked. The angel answered, 'Your prayers and gifts to the poor have come up as a memorial offering before God.'"

—ACTS 10:4

Have you ever given a gift to someone—especially someone who was in need—and felt like it wasn't appreciated? Or worse, like it was wasted? A rejected, unappreciated, or wasted gift can discourage us from giving in the future. What's the point, after all, if our gift is just going to be discarded?

But we should never tire of giving generously, whether we have a little or a lot from which to give. However our gifts are received by those we give them to, God sees our generosity. God knows every sacrifice you've made to help someone else. God knows each time you've put another's needs above your own. And those are memorial offerings before God.

And even if it *seems* like your gifts go unnoticed, you never know what seeds you're planting in someone else with your generosity. Keep giving!

DAY 211

"And he blessed Abram, saying, 'Blessed be Abram by God Most High, Creator of heaven and earth. And praise be to God Most High, who delivered your enemies into your hand.' Then Abram gave him a tenth of everything."

—GENESIS 14:19–20

Tithing is an interesting concept. This little passage from Genesis shows Abram's interaction with Melchizedek. Abram suddenly gives a tenth of everything to this mysterious man. Later, the concept of tithing was locked into the law given to Moses (Leviticus 27:30–34). And finally, in Hebrews 7, Paul discusses old covenant tithing and the new covenant priesthood in the "order of Melchizedek."

There is some debate about how to properly interpret Hebrews 7, whether or not it is a directive for new covenant Christians to tithe in the same way the law demands. But whether or not we're commanded to tithe, one thing is certain. We're commanded to be deeply and consistently generous, and that includes supporting ministries at our local church and helping the poor and the overlooked. Give freely and often!

DAY 212

"Woe to you Pharisees, because you give God a tenth of your mint, rue and all other kinds of garden herbs, but you neglect justice and the love of God. You should have practiced the latter without leaving the former undone."

—LUKE 11:42

If the Pharisees were giving their tithes, as the law commanded, what was the problem? Why did Jesus rebuke them? Jesus acknowledged the Pharisees tithing was a good thing, but they had completely missed the entire spirit of the law. They didn't love and care for the people. They added heavy tradition-based burdens to the law. And above all, they glorified themselves and sought their own desires instead of God's. Otherwise, they might have known Jesus as Messiah when they saw him.

We should take Jesus's rebuke to the Pharisees to heart for ourselves. Writing huge checks to various ministries isn't the point of our generosity. No, the point of our giving is to show true, sacrificial love to others—to show that we value the needs of others above our own. Keep that spirit at the heart of all your giving!

DAY 213

"He is the Rock, his works are perfect, and all his ways are just. A faithful God who does no wrong, upright and just is he."

—DEUTERONOMY 32:4

When we think of our God being a God of justice, it may bring to mind some scary images. We think of justice as being punishment for wrongdoing, and that is part of the word's meaning. But the words translated as "justice" and "righteousness" in English are part of the same word family in both Hebrew and Greek. When we consider the original languages of the Bible, we can get a clearer picture of what a "just" God actually looks like—and it's not a big angry God waiting to toss lightning bolts at us.

God's justice is intertwined with his righteousness. God always does right. And he is the final standard of what's right and what's wrong. Unlike our human systems of justice, God's justice is perfect and it's always built upon what is truly right. While our own imperfection can sometimes make us fear God's perfect justice, we can rest in the knowledge that his justice is always good, fair, and laced with grace.

DAY 214

"Do not take revenge, my dear friends, but leave room for God's wrath, for it is written: 'It is mine to avenge; I will repay,' says the Lord."

—ROMANS 12:19

In theory, we should always be able to trust those closest to us. Our family, our best friends, our boyfriends—these are the people we should be able to count on no matter what . . . right? So what happens when our BFF morphs from "best friend forever" to "backstabbing former friend"?

When given the opportunity, sometimes we would love to take revenge on those who betray us. We may even feel justified in our revenge when they were in the wrong and we were truly innocent.

But God tells us to avoid taking revenge. It's not that he doesn't see our pain. Of course he does, and when his children are suffering unfairly, you better believe that bothers God as much as it bothers us. But vengeance belongs to God. Only he sees situations perfectly clearly. He is the only one who can rightly judge each of us—not only those who have hurt us, but you and me too! Instead, let's try to bear slights with grace and patience and let God sort out the guilt or innocence of others.

DAY 215

"God presented Christ as a sacrifice of atonement, through the shedding of his blood—to be received by faith. He did this to demonstrate his righteousness, because in his forbearance he had left the sins committed beforehand unpunished—he did it to demonstrate his righteousness at the present time, so as to be just and the one who justifies those who have faith in Jesus."

—ROMANS 3:25–26

It's natural to feel fear when we think about God's plan to punish sin. God wouldn't be just if he didn't do what's right—that is, punish sins against him. So the idea of God's need to punish every instance of sin rightfully freaks us out.

But God's justice is central to the Gospel of grace and really should strike us with wonder, not terror. Instead of punishing us for every one of our sins, God sent Jesus Christ to take the once-and-for-all punishment for *all* sins. God needs to punish sin, yes. But instead of obliterating humanity, he used a sinless substitution. Instead of simply being punished *by* him, we are able to have a loving relationship *with* him. And that was God's design for humankind all along.

So let's give thanks for the awesome lengths to which God has gone to restore his relationship with us while fulfilling his ultimate need for justice.

DAY 216

"But who are you, a human being, to talk back to God? 'Shall what is formed say to the one who formed it, "Why did you make me like this?"' Does not the potter have the right to make out of the same lump of clay some pottery for special purposes and some for common use?"

—ROMANS 9:20–21

In many cultures throughout all history, human independence has been highly valued. Independence, free-thinking, and self-sufficiency can be wonderful, positive traits in many ways. But those traits can also rub up against our faith, causing friction and lack of growth.

When it comes down to it, recognizing God's righteousness requires us to humble ourselves. We have to acknowledge that God and his Word are our ultimate standard of right and wrong. But we want to make our own judgment calls. We don't want to take the time to analyze all the "gray areas" that the Bible might not mention directly. And sometimes, we flat-out want to argue with what we know God wants us to do because it conflicts with our desires.

But Paul's words here can be summed up simply: He's God; we're not. It may be hard for our independence to accept it sometimes, but this simple act of humility will lead to better, wiser choices and softer hearts, more open to God's leading in our lives.

DAY 217

"If we confess our sins, he is faithful and just and will forgive us our sins and purify us from all unrighteousness."

—1 JOHN 1:9

One of the hardest things in the world is admitting we are wrong. "I made a mistake. I messed up. I made the wrong choice." Why are those things so incredibly hard to say? Pride might have something to do with it. But it might also be fear. Sometimes it's easier to pretend we never messed up than it is to face the consequences of our wrongdoing.

But we can't dodge God so easily. He already knows all the wrong we've done. Eep! Does that make anyone else want to run and hide? But when we're followers of Jesus, we don't need to be scared of confession.

While we still have to deal with worldly consequences of our sin, like apologizing for feelings we've hurt or accepting punishments for rules we've broken, we are not condemned by our sin. Jesus took care of that for us. God's justice has been satisfied, so the process of confession is about humility and growth. It brings us closer to God and allows us to experience his forgiveness. It also strengthens our relationships with others when we build our bonds on honesty.

DAY 218

"I have not spoken in secret, from somewhere in a land of darkness; I have not said to Jacob's descendants, 'Seek me in vain.' I, the Lord, speak the truth; I declare what is right."

—ISAIAH 45:19

The world can be a confusing place. In some ways, it'd be nice if we lived in the exact culture of the ancient Israelites so we could directly apply the ins and outs of God's Word to our lives. On the other hand, it's pretty nice to have cars and electricity and glitter and mascara.

While there are many excellent luxuries that come with living in modern times, one drawback is we have a ton of aspects of our lives that aren't spoken of directly in the Bible. How does God feel about modern technology? What types of entertainment should we avoid, if any? What should our modern worship services look like? These are just a few of the hundreds, if not thousands, of questions a modern Christian might have that aren't directly addressed in the Bible.

But God does reveal himself—his heart, his will—to us in his Word. He equips us with his Word and his Spirit to guide us in these gray areas. With these tools in our spiritual tool belt, we can still look to God as our final standard of right and wrong. All while enjoying our electricity.

DAY 219

"'I have the right to do anything,' you say—but not everything is beneficial."

—1 CORINTHIANS 6:12A

God has given us the great gift of free will. But sometimes—er, maybe oftentimes—that free will gets us in trouble because we make wrong choices. There is also a theological error that says "Let's sin big every once in a while, just to thumb our noses at Satan because we live under grace!" Paul warns against such things in his letters to the brand-new Christian churches of the first century. And with good reason.

Today, we still struggle with these wonky ideas of grace and free will. When navigating the gray areas of our world, it's very important that we take care to make good choices that God would approve. In the theological sense, we have the "right" to do anything because Jesus has saved us. But Paul warns the Corinthians (and us!) that not everything is good for us. We shouldn't do whatever we want because we can cause harm to others, ourselves, and the church.

Jesus paid a hefty price on the cross. We need to live our lives in such a way that we don't mock that sacrifice. Live freely, but wisely!

DAY 220

"'I have the right to do anything'—but I will not be mastered by anything."

—1 CORINTHIANS 6:12B

Sometimes our gray-area situations in life start out as something that could be described as beneficial. Working hard to achieve our goals in school and work, for example, is a good thing. But letting our ambitions swallow us to the point that we're willing to sacrifice our relationships with God and others is not. Enjoying the wonderful food and drink we have available to us is a good thing. But becoming addicted to alcohol or junk food to the point that it destroys our lives or our health is not.

So even beyond asking if a gray-area situation is potentially beneficial, we also need to ask ourselves if we've crossed a line into allowing something other than God to master us. We cannot serve two masters in our lives—God and something else (Matthew 6:24). We can only properly serve one master, and that master should be God.

DAY 221

"Be careful, however, that the exercise of your rights does not become a stumbling block to the weak. For if someone with a weak conscience sees you, with all your knowledge, eating in an idol's temple, won't that person be emboldened to eat what is sacrificed to idols? So this weak brother or sister, for whom Christ died, is destroyed by your knowledge."

—1 CORINTHIANS 8:9–11

If we have a gray-area situation we've determined is beneficial and has not become an unhealthy master over us, are we totally in the clear? Not necessarily. God also wants us to consider others in the choices we make.

We have a responsibility to our fellow believers. Maybe we have a new-believer friend who was previously addicted to Instagram and she's trying to cut it out of her life to better focus on her relationship with God. Using Instagram isn't a sin, but if we flaunt our use of Instagram in this friend's face, we're becoming a potential stumbling block for her. In some ways, that sounds crazy. If it's not a sin, aren't we allowed to do it? In theory, yes. But not if it's going to spiritually or morally harm a fellow believer.

This really comes down to putting others before ourselves, which is a principle we see often throughout the Bible. When deciding if something is right or wrong in God's eyes, we must consider those around us.

DAY 222

"So whether you eat or drink or whatever you do, do it all for the glory of God."

—1 CORINTHIANS 10:31

Giving glory to God is a phrase we hear a lot. But have we ever really thought about what it means? To glorify God is to acknowledge his greatness—to be aware of his splendor. We glorify God when we speak well of him, tell others about his greatness, and offer our lives as sacrifices to him. So when we're trying to decide whether something is right or wrong in God's sight, we can ask ourselves if this decision will draw attention to God's greatness or subtract from it. Will it help us show God's character to the world or hinder its understanding of him?

The world is complex and can be scary at times. But God has given us all the tools we need to discern his standard of right and wrong, even as we deal with the murky gray areas of life. Don't be afraid to use them!

DAY 223

"But the Israelites said to the Lord, 'We have sinned. Do with us whatever you think best, but please rescue us now.'"

—JUDGES 10:15

One of the clearest pictures we can get of God's character is when we look at the perfect harmony of God's justice and mercy. Like the Israelites at the time of the judges, we ask God to judge us rightly (justice), but also to rescue us from ourselves (mercy).

And the coolest part is that God's character insists he do both things. He judges us rightly, according to his ultimate standard of right and wrong. But he also rescues us—offers us forgiveness, grace, and reconciliation, even when he has judged us to have sinned. These two attributes of God balance so exactly, they're like two sides of the same coin. We can't consider one without the other. If we do, our picture of God will be incomplete.

DAY 224

"May the Lord *repay you for what you have done. May you be richly rewarded by the* Lord, *the God of Israel, under whose wings you have come to take refuge."*

—RUTH 2:12

What we do matters to God. Sometimes people misunderstand the idea of grace and believe that our thoughts, words, and actions aren't of much concern to God, since we're saved by grace through faith. And part of that is true—we are absolutely saved by grace through faith. But the other part? Not so much.

Our actions are important to God. Our words are important to God. And even our deepest, most secret thoughts are important to God. That's why we have so many guidelines in the Bible. Our behavior—good and bad, right and wrong—makes a difference. And in God's great generosity, he rewards our good deeds and faithfulness in multiple ways. There are heavenly rewards like those mentioned in Luke 6:35 and Ephesians 6:8. And our good deeds often have rewards here on earth too. Those rewards can come in the form of strengthened relationships with others, excellent reputations, or even just the deep satisfaction that comes from knowing we're serving God in a way that pleases him!

DAY 225

"In everything set them an example by doing what is good. In your teaching show integrity, seriousness and soundness of speech that cannot be condemned, so that those who oppose you may be ashamed because they have nothing bad to say about us."

—TITUS 2:7–8

If our good deeds matter to God, what sort of good deeds does he want us to do? If we wrote a list of all the good deeds we could possibly do that would please God, it'd probably be long enough to wrap around the globe. Twice. There's no shortage of good a follower of Jesus can do in this life to love her neighbor.

And here in Titus we have but one example of a good work that glorifies God—using "speech that cannot be condemned." In other words, using words that no one can find fault with. Whoa. In this day and age where there's at least one person on the Internet offended by *everything*?

Before speaking, we need to pause, think, and reflect. Before posting things on social media for all the world to see, we need to pause, think, and reflect. Are our words worthy of our high calling? Are we speaking serious, sound truth, or just sounding off? Do good by seriously considering your words—before they're said.

"Religion that God our Father accepts as pure and faultless is this: to look after orphans and widows in their distress and to keep oneself from being polluted by the world."

—JAMES 1:27

This is a great verse about good works. It's a fabulous "put your money where your mouth is" sort of a verse. Except we're not talking about literal money. We're talking about care for others. James says that pure, faultless religion acceptable to God isn't centered around fancy liturgy or a loud, public show of prayer and "righteousness," like the sort of religion the Pharisees practiced.

No, the religion God accepts is that of looking after widows and orphans—the most distressed of the world. Those who don't know where their next meal will come from. Those whose place in society is unsure. Those who are overlooked, abandoned, and oppressed. Caring for these, the "least" of us, is the sort of religion our Lord wants from us. It's pure and unpolluted by the world. If you're looking for a place to start in your good deeds, look no further than the many ministries that reach out to the most vulnerable people—or start your own!

DAY 227

"What good is it, my brothers and sisters, if someone claims to have faith but has no deeds? Can such faith save them? Suppose a brother or a sister is without clothes and daily food. If one of you says to them, "Go in peace; keep warm and well fed," but does nothing about their physical needs, what good is it? In the same way, faith by itself, if it is not accompanied by action, is dead."

—JAMES 2:14–17

James is a great book to read if you're looking for ways to actively live out your faith. Here James stresses the importance of deeds, firstly, and then he mentions something specific that followers of Jesus can do to live out their faith—giving generously to those in need.

It's vitally important that followers of Christ share their faith and the Gospel message with others. Spiritual life is on the line, after all. But it's also vitally important that Christians care for the physical, worldly needs of others too. When people see Christians volunteer at a shelter, build homes on a mission trip, or help out within their communities, they can see our words in action. They can *see* the love we speak of when we share it with them in practical, tangible ways.

DAY 228

"Learn to do right; seek justice. Defend the oppressed. Take up the cause of the fatherless; plead the case of the widow."

—ISAIAH 1:17

You would think in the nearly three thousand years since the book of Isaiah was written, we might have figured out how to do away with oppression. That humankind would have "learned to do right," as the book says. But oppression still exists, even in the most advanced societies. Oppression and injustice will always exist in some form until God creates the world anew and sin is finally defeated for good.

But that doesn't mean we give up. Those who love Jesus should be at the forefront of defending the weak and the oppressed. Those who love Jesus should be known for their unceasing work in caring for those who are rejected or persecuted by their society. It was necessary in Isaiah's time. It was necessary in Jesus's time. And it's every bit as necessary in our time.

DAY 229

"He said to them, 'Go into all the world and preach the gospel to all creation.'"

—MARK 16:15

The ultimate of all the good deeds a follower of Jesus can do is to tell others about our savior's work of salvation on the cross. Physical needs matter. Speaking out against injustice and oppression matters. But if we've done every good earthly work while failing to tell others about God's salvation, we've missed the most important point.

Each person's time on earth is short compared to eternity. That means the soul must be our main focus even as we continue to meet earthly needs and fight for justice in this lifetime. Jesus came to earth and died on the cross to save our souls. It was the very core of his human existence, and once we believe in him, it becomes the very core of our existence too. It's impossible for us *not* to share the source of our salvation with others.

DAY 230

"Sing to God, sing in praise of his name, extol him who rides on the clouds; rejoice before him—his name is the LORD. A father to the fatherless, a defender of widows, is God in his holy dwelling."

—PSALM 68:4–5

Reflecting God's justice means we have to fight for those God fights for. Our society is different than those in the Bible. It's different than ancient Israel, and it's different than Judea and Greece under Roman rule. So while Scripture frequently mentions caring for the fatherless and the widow, those are only two of many people groups God especially wants his people to care for.

Why was there so much concern for the fatherless and the widow in ancient Israel, Judea, and Greece? In those societies—patriarchal and based heavily on farming and trade—a child without a father and a woman without a husband were at a serious disadvantage. They were the most vulnerable members of society, along with the "alien" or foreigner, also mentioned many times in Scripture.

So who are our widows, orphans, and aliens? Single parents, children in foster care, refugees, immigrants, those facing racism, those facing persecution . . . the list goes on. Every society has those who are vulnerable, and God has always cared for these people. Likewise, he commands his followers to care for them too. What can you do today to help?

DAY 231

"They claim to know God, but by their actions they deny him. They are detestable, disobedient and unfit for doing anything good."

—TITUS 1:16

If those who love Jesus seek to reflect God's righteous justice, it is vitally important we avoid hypocrisy. Christians get accused of hypocrisy a lot, of talking the talk but not walking the walk. It's easy for us to dismiss such accusations as unfair persecution. And sometimes, they certainly are.

But it's important that we don't mistakenly believe ourselves to be above hypocrisy, just because some of the accusations leveled at us may be untrue. Jesus's most repeated complaint against the Pharisees was that they were hypocrites. So it certainly matters to God that we don't say we believe in a biblical moral code and then practice something else entirely in real life. That's what hypocrisy is—a disconnect between your stated beliefs and your behavior.

We all mess up sometimes. That's being imperfect, not a hypocrite. Hypocrisy is claiming to love Jesus while consistently acting in an unloving manner toward God or others. It's saying you are one thing—a follower of Jesus Christ—while acting in the opposite manner he'd want you to. We must make every effort to avoid this. If we fall into hypocrisy, we fail to reflect our God of righteous justice.

"The King is mighty, he loves justice—you have established equity; in Jacob you have done what is just and right."

—PSALM 99:4

Prejudice is a big buzzword these days. It has been for many decades, as our society struggles to figure out civil rights for women, ethnic minorities, and many other people groups. Throughout history, the struggle to overcome the prejudice of others has been seen in the demand for voting rights, the fight against racial discrimination, and even the battle for physical freedom. Prejudice has been buzzing for a long time.

But in order for us to fully embrace true fairness, we need the sort of perspective God has. Fairness is not always about sameness. It's not about pretending genders are exactly the same or there are no cultural differences between ethnicities. True fairness is about even judgment, free of bias. It's about moving past surface differences straight to a person's heart, just as God does. It's not that the differences don't exist. It's that they don't play into God's assessment of a person. That's true justice—true equity. And that's what God's people should strive for in their dealings with others, especially those who look and think differently than we do.

DAY 233

"So God said to him, 'Since you have asked for this and not for long life or wealth for yourself, nor have asked for the death of your enemies but for discernment in administering justice, I will do what you have asked. I will give you a wise and discerning heart, so that there will never have been anyone like you, nor will there ever be.'"

—1 KINGS 3:11–12

Since we do not possess God's perfect knowledge or perfect righteousness, it would be easy to say we should never seek justice, since we can't practice it perfectly the way God does. And we do need to be very careful to avoid becoming judgmental rather than just.

But for most people, there is a time in their lives when they are put in a position of authority, whether it's as a parent, teacher, boss, or even as an elected official. And it is deeply important that authority figures seek justice. It is right, good, and godly for a person in authority to echo Solomon's prayer to God. When facing the reality of becoming king over Israel, Solomon did not ask for worldly riches but for wisdom to lead the people well. And God gave it to him in abundance so that he might administer proper justice.

We can (and should!) make the same request of God when we find ourselves in authority positions. Seek true justice and love what's right.

DAY 234

"Blessed are you when people insult you, persecute you and falsely say all kinds of evil against you because of me. Rejoice and be glad, because great is your reward in heaven, for in the same way they persecuted the prophets who were before you."

—MATTHEW 5:11–12

Have you ever found yourself on the receiving end of injustice? Have you ever been in a situation that was totally, utterly unfair?

That's hardly even a question, right? We have *all* found ourselves in situations that are unfair, and we will all face unfair situations in the future. As we've probably heard more than once, that's life! So, when we face these unfair situations, how are we supposed to react? How do we respond to unfairness directed our way?

Jesus says we're blessed by mistreatment. What! How can that possibly be true? But that's what he says, very plainly. And that's because mistreatment gives us the opportunity to reflect Jesus's character. Like him, we can stand firm in our faith in God. We can continue to love our enemies and show grace to those who only want to show us scorn. Practicing what we preach builds our faith and our character.

DAY 235

"If your brother or sister sins, go and point out their fault, just between the two of you. If they listen to you, you have won them over. But if they will not listen, take one or two others along, so that 'every matter may be established by the testimony of two or three witnesses.' If they still refuse to listen, tell it to the church; and if they refuse to listen even to the church, treat them as you would a pagan or a tax collector."

—MATTHEW 18:15–17

Conflict happens. We wish it didn't but unfortunately, that's not realistic. Relationships face pressure, and sometimes friendships are shattered.

Ouch. It hurts even to write it. As much as we love Jesus and as much as we want to do right, sometimes we fall short. And people can get hurt in the process. Thankfully, there's a biblical method for dealing with it when a brother or sister in Christ sins against us. And mercifully, it doesn't have to involve cutting your friend out of your life.

Biblical methods of dealing with conflict almost always put restoration first. The first and most important step is to address your friend directly. How often do we miss this step? How often do we go speak to a third party to "vent" before speaking directly to the one who hurt us? There are more steps if this first proves unsuccessful, but in many situations, open, loving communication is all that's needed.

DAY 236

"Those who hate me without reason outnumber the hairs of my head; many are my enemies without cause, those who seek to destroy me. I am forced to restore what I did not steal."

—PSALM 69:4

Sometimes, much to our chagrin, there's nothing we can do about injustice against us. Sometimes, there's no action we can take, no reconciliation to be found, no higher cause to point to. Unfairness happens. And it stinks.

It can be extremely difficult to set aside our desire to see things set right, especially when we're the ones who are being treated unfairly. But when these inevitable situations crash down on us, we can take refuge in the fact that God sees us. God hears us. God know the truth, and God is not swayed by others' opinions of us. He loves, champions, and supports his children, even when the world doesn't. *Especially* when the world doesn't.

So, when the world hands us the short end of the stick, we don't despair. We lean harder into our savior and know that in the end, we will be vindicated.

DAY 237

"Brothers and sisters, do not slander one another. Anyone who speaks against a brother or sister or judges them speaks against the law and judges it. When you judge the law, you are not keeping it, but sitting in judgment on it. There is only one Lawgiver and Judge, the one who is able to save and destroy. But you—who are you to judge your neighbor?"

—JAMES 4:11–12

While seeking to reflect God's righteous justice, it's important that we keep words like these from James in mind. It is right and noble to pursue justice for others, but we must remember our proper role.

Only God has the authority to judge or condemn. The word "judge" causes confusion sometimes. Sometimes people wrongly assume that since we're not to judge, we have no authority to say what's right or wrong. But that's not the sort of judgment the Bible is talking about. We not only have the right but the mandate to *discern* right from wrong. That sort of judgment is how we steer clear of false teachers, recognize true fellow believers, and avoid unbiblical teachings.

What we don't have the right to do is condemn anyone. Judgment—the sort that looks straight to the soul of a person and determines her heart and her eternal position—belongs *only* to God. He is the only one equipped to make that call.

DAY 238

"So when you, a mere human being, pass judgment on them and yet do the same things, do you think you will escape God's judgment?"

—ROMANS 2:3

God sees through a lens of clearest crystal. There is nothing to obscure his vision, nothing to darken his view, nothing to bias him in one direction or another. If only we could say the same.

Unfortunately, our human weakness shows itself here. Again. Our lenses are clouded. Our eyes are even blinded at times. And more often than we'd like, we have a speck of sin—or even a plank of sin—stuck in our eyes, blocking our vision. Our point-of-view is imperfect, and that can skew our judgment of people and situations.

So what can we do about it? Being aware of our own sin—sin that obscures our vision—is a great first step. We can also pray for ever-increasing wisdom and discernment to know what is right and to pursue justice the way God wants us to.

DAY 239

"Do not pervert justice; do not show partiality to the poor or favoritism to the great, but judge your neighbor fairly."

—LEVITICUS 19:15

When justice is mishandled, it is an offense to God. If that language seems too strong, think of all the many verses in the Bible that mention justice, impartiality (that is, fairness), and righteousness. These things are important to God. If they weren't, his book wouldn't talk about them so much!

Because these things are important to God, we should pay special attention to them. They should be important to us. We want to avoid offending God, definitely, but we also recognize everything that matters to God matters to him for a reason. A focus on justice, fairness, and righteousness brings glory to God. It builds his kingdom. And these pursuits help us grow spiritually as individuals. Caring about the things close to God's heart is always a benefit to us, those around us, and the world.

DAY 240

"Can someone who hates justice govern? Will you condemn the just and mighty One? Is he not the One who says to kings, 'You are worthless,' and to nobles, 'You are wicked,' who shows no partiality to princes and does not favor the rich over the poor, for they are all the work of his hands?"

—JOB 34: 17–19

Every person matters to God. Every life matters to God. A soul is not less worthy to him because it doesn't meet some worldly standard of wealth, beauty, intelligence, or talent. God sees hearts, and all those hearts matter to him.

That's because the rich and the poor, the privileged and the persecuted, the disadvantaged and the advantaged, the disabled and the able are all created by God in his image. The lives of every people group—each minority and majority—are important to him. In a world that seems so sharply divided along lines of gender, race, culture, nationality, and religion, it's important that we hear this message over and over. We need to be reminded how little these lines mean to our God. He desires *all* people be drawn to him through a relationship with Jesus Christ. May we endeavor to show that same sort of love to others on God's behalf.

DAY 241

"I am the Lord, *the God of all mankind. Is anything too hard for me?"*

—JEREMIAH 32:27

Omnipotence is a big word with a simple meaning. *Omni* means "all," and *potens* means "powerful." So when we say God is omnipotent, it means he is all-powerful. Thanks for being simple, Latin!

The concept of God's omnipotence is so central to his character he is even called the Almighty. His power is pointed out in that name. And that's because that's who he is—the Lord who is full of authority and ability. When we speak of God's omnipotence, we mean that he is able to do his holy will in its entirety. That's a big, powerful God we serve.

God's omnipotence—his great ability and power—was often the attribute pointed out when God was being compared to the worthless gods the Israelites were so prone to idolize. God's power makes him unique. God's power makes him real.

DAY 242

"And do not think you can say to yourselves, 'We have Abraham as our father.' I tell you that out of these stones God can raise up children for Abraham."

—MATTHEW 3:9

Sometimes we see people who are super-wealthy or have massive celebrity status, and it seems like they are so powerful, they rule the world. We also have the equivalent in our personal lives. Maybe a really popular guy or girl at school whose word is like law.

For those of us who find ourselves outside of this "power status" group, it's easy to feel very small and insignificant. But when we compare the worldly power of these folks with the utter awesomeness of God's power, we find there's no real comparison at all. All of the social status, money, or even physical prowess in the world doesn't measure up to God's strength. And that's the God who sees us, knows us, and loves us.

We never need to feel small, insignificant, or intimidated by others. We have a very powerful God on our side. And, as influential as some people may appear at times, God is truly the one who wields the power of the world.

DAY 243

"If we are faithless, he remains faithful, for he cannot disown himself."

—2 TIMOTHY 2:13

Is there anything God can't do? It seems like the right thing to say would be "Of course not! God can do anything!"

But this isn't the complete picture. We have to add a small caveat to that statement—small, but important. God cannot do anything that goes against his character. God cannot deny himself.

So . . . what does that even mean? What sort of limitations are put on God, and why should it matter to us? God can't sin. He can't change. He can't cease to be loving, just, holy, wise, all-knowing, or all-powerful—and that's a good thing! This means the God of the Bible is still the God we love today. It means his promises won't fail. It means he'll never make a mistake or do something bad. We should praise God that there is this no limit to his power because it makes him, our foundation, totally secure.

DAY 244

"The Lord turned to him and said, 'Go in the strength you have and save Israel out of Midian's hand. Am I not sending you?'"

—JUDGES 6:14

Like all of God's attributes, God's power is a trait his human creations get to reflect in some way. God's power, of course, far exceeds ours, but we get some measure of power in different areas of our lives. Our physical bodies are one such way God's strength is reflected in us.

Some people are gifted with incredible strength and physical prowess. Have you ever stood next to a professional football player? Wow! Those guys are huge and powerful. Some people have been gifted with hands that do incredible work—flying across a piano keyboard, hand-stitching detailed embroidery, painting great works of art, or crafting furniture out of raw wood. Those are all amazing feats of our physical bodies. Some legs are blessed for extraordinary dancing, some voices for angelic singing. Though we may be gifted differently, and able in varying degrees, just the functionality of our internal organs is a reflection of God's power. Our physical bodies are exceptional gifts!

DAY 245

"He will be the sure foundation for your times, a rich store of salvation and wisdom and knowledge; the fear of the LORD is the key to this treasure."

—ISAIAH 33:6

An even greater blessing than physical strength is God's power reflected through our mental strength. The human mind is an incredible thing—complex and full of great depth. Modern neuroscience is a comparatively young science, and researchers have only begun to scratch the surface of unlocking the human mind. What an incredible testimony to the One who created our brains!

We reflect God in our wisdom, knowledge, and intelligence. But we also reflect him in our ability to mentally withstand suffering. It is often said that the human spirit is "resilient"—meaning our emotional state rebounds from trauma, suffering, and unimaginable circumstances. And this is because our minds are mirroring the power and strength of the one who designed them.

Have you ever felt like something you're dealing with emotionally has "broken" you? Be encouraged! Not only are you not alone, but you are made of some incredibly strong building blocks.

DAY 246

"Paul entered the synagogue and spoke boldly there for three months, arguing persuasively about the kingdom of God."

—ACTS 19:8

Ever heard the phrase "the power of persuasion"? Being able to present one's case with clear, logical, well-positioned reasoning is a valuable skill. And one that may drive your parents crazy sometimes.

Being a persuasive speaker can be a great benefit when discussing serious subjects like politics and current events. And it's certainly essential if you have a career in law! But truly the best application of this sort of power is using it the way Paul did as a traveling missionary. He used his powers of persuasion to boldly proclaim the Gospel. He used his power to present a compelling case for Jesus Christ as the Son of God who died for mankind's sins and made a way to salvation. He convinced people of these truths.

We each may or may not be called to do the sort of work Paul did. But we are each called to have a ready answer when people ask us about our faith. Think about your responses to those kinds of questions so you won't be caught off-guard if, and when, you're asked.

DAY 247

"Coral and jasper are not worthy of mention; the price of wisdom is beyond rubies."

—JOB 28:18

Some of us are called to positions of power and authority in the world. Those positions may be in government, or they may be in business. Perhaps they are positions of power within a ministry. Whether these positions of authority are in organizations large or small, followers of Jesus can have a great impact on the people around them when God sees to it that they're placed in positions of influence.

And it's extremely important that, when we find ourselves in positions of power and authority, we use this power wisely and well, as God would want us to. The foundation of using authority well is wisdom. Our decisions—and even our thoughts and words—must be grounded in wisdom. Social power, power in business, and power in ministry can lead to corruption. When we become addicted to authority, we no longer give glory to the one who placed us in authority in the first place. God is our source, and it's crucial we all remember that—even more so the ones who are called to exercise authority over others.

DAY 248

"But we have this treasure in jars of clay to show that this all-surpassing power is from God and not from us."
—2 CORINTHIANS 4:7

Perhaps the clearest reflection of God's power within us is in the spiritual power we possess. The disciples were able to perform miracles in Jesus's name. God empowered his chosen ones like Moses and Elijah to accomplish amazing feats. And every follower of Jesus is empowered to pray in faith, to show great acts of love, to have peace, joy, and perseverance that defy all reason. This is our spiritual power.

And perhaps the reason these gifts seem such a clear reflection of God is because it's not truly on our own power that we are able to do such things. Our spiritual power is God's power shining through us. We're the small, humble "jars of clay." God uses us in our weakness to better display his power. And sometimes that power is *best* displayed through the cracks in our ability and strength. Where we are weak, he is strong.

DAY 249

"I will give you hidden treasures, riches stored in secret places, so that you may know that I am the Lord, *the God of Israel, who summons you by name."*

—ISAIAH 45:3

Our free will is a treasure. God certainly has the power to force everyone to do exactly what he wants them to. But instead, he gives us a great gift. God allows us to make choices in our lives—to choose friends, careers, where we want to live, how we like to dress, what we want to eat, which church we'd like to attend. This is a power we are given in our lives, and we must choose to use it wisely.

Some of the choices we can make may sound like small, insignificant things. Does it really matter if we choose oatmeal over toast for breakfast? But when any of those choices is taken away, whether by illness, financial concerns, oppression, or some other circumstance, we begin to see what a blessing our ability to make choices—even the small ones—truly is.

DAY 250

"Then God said, 'Let us make mankind in our image, in our likeness, so that they may rule over the fish in the sea and the birds in the sky, over the livestock and all the wild animals, and over all the creatures that move along the ground.'"

—GENESIS 1:26

Mankind's free will is one of our most godlike traits. Like the ability to create things, our ability to choose is like the giant thumbprint of God, stamped on each of us. These are the parts of humanity that set us above the rest of God's beautiful creation and caused him to declare that we were made in his image.

Having the power to choose means we can also choose wrong. That's what makes choices so scary sometimes. We can, and do, make bad ones, and bad choices almost always have unpleasant consequences.

But we shouldn't let fear of bad choices keep us from recognizing the great gift of choice God has given us. We have many guidelines within Scripture to help us make good choices in our lives, and if we hold to those guidelines, we don't need to fear God's gift of choice.

DAY 251

"For we must all appear before the judgment seat of Christ, so that each of us may receive what is due us for the things done while in the body, whether good or bad."

—2 CORINTHIANS 5:10

Theologians and scholars have been debating about free will for centuries, and they're not likely to stop any time soon. How much free will do humans have? How does God's rule come into play? If we affirm one too heavily, do we incorrectly neglect the other?

Whatever questions surround free will, one thing is sure: our choices matter to God. As much as we know our bad choices displease God, the reverse is also true. When we make wise decisions and when we sacrifice for others (aka display true love), God is very pleased with us.

That's because when we make good choices, we're exercising our free will the way it was intended to be used. Before sin entered the equation, mankind always exercised free will in a way that pleased God. Make every effort to honor God in your choices today and each day.

DAY 252

"I pray that out of his glorious riches he may strengthen you with power through his Spirit in your inner being."

—EPHESIANS 3:16

God's great power isn't just about huge feats of cosmic importance. Certainly God does huge, cosmic things, too, but he's also a personal God and a God of small details.

Have you ever felt completely overworked at school? Have you ever been completely stressed about a fight with a friend? Or maybe you've been butting heads with your parents, just not able to see eye-to-eye lately. These things can make us feel emotionally, physically, and spiritually exhausted. When we're exhausted, we need a strong support system to sustain us. And, amazingly, our powerful God cares about these details.

As much as we may think what we want most is complete independence and strength within ourselves, having the all-powerful God of everything as our support system—like a spine made of steel—is not only a comforting thought. It's an empowering one.

DAY 253

"The Sovereign LORD is my strength; he makes my feet like the feet of a deer, he enables me to tread on the heights."

—HABAKKUK 3:19

It would be easy to mistakenly think that God's power being so huge somehow diminishes our power. That because his power is nearly infinite, it means ours is nonexistent. But that's just not an idea supported by Scripture. In fact, God's power enables us.

It is God's power that created us in the first place. It is God's power that brought us from death to life through Jesus Christ. It will be by God's power that Christ returns and we are resurrected to spend eternity on a new earth—a new earth God creates by (wait for it) his power! In God's great power, we have life, salvation, ability, and the freedom to do everything God calls us to do.

God doesn't use his power to squash and suppress us. He uses his great power to enable us to serve him.

DAY 254

"I have told you these things, so that in me you may have peace. In this world you will have trouble. But take heart! I have overcome the world."

—JOHN 16:33

A phrase repeated so often that it's become a bit of a cliché is "peace which transcends all understanding" or "peace that passes understanding" (Philippians 4:7). There's a reason many Bible verses or Christianese sayings have become clichés—it's because they're great verses full of truth! And this case is no exception.

Trouble is promised to everyone in this life, and especially to Christians as we battle our selfish desires and try to become more like Jesus. And sometimes trouble comes as the world battles us to try to silence God's message. But we shouldn't let this scare us. God's great power spills into his people to create peace that makes no earthly sense. That's what peace which transcends all understanding means. It's a peace that is beyond reason because it comes directly from God's power spilling into us.

As Jesus said, we should take heart. The world will throw hardship at us, but Jesus has overcome the world, and in that knowledge, we have supernatural peace.

DAY 255

"Our God, will you not judge them? For we have no power to face this vast army that is attacking us. We do not know what to do, but our eyes are on you."

—2 CHRONICLES 20:12

One of the worst feelings in the world is being powerless. Facing impossible odds. Being hemmed in, held down, pressed upon. When we're powerless, we become easy victims for those who would prey on us. And this is one reason God has put so many mandates in Scripture to protect the weakest members of society. But what about when we *are* the weak ones?

Take heart. Being powerless—and indeed being victimized by someone else—does *not* mean God has abandoned you. It does not mean God is judging or punishing you. Powerlessness and victimization are realities we deal with because our world is sinful. Even if we do everything "perfectly," we may find ourselves in such a situation because someone else is choosing to dishonor God.

But God holds the weak and the powerless close to himself. We can fall back on our knowledge that God's love is sure. God will not leave us. And in the end, God will be the judge of all people—not just us, but those who would seek to take advantage of the vulnerable.

DAY 256

"Praise be to the God and Father of our Lord Jesus Christ, the Father of compassion and the God of all comfort, who comforts us in all our troubles, so that we can comfort those in any trouble with the comfort we ourselves receive from God."

—2 CORINTHIANS 1:3–4

If our ability reflects God's power, what does it mean when we begin to lose some of those abilities? Or, perhaps, if we're born without certain abilities at all? That's certainly a scary reality to be facing. And oftentimes, the loss of ability comes in a sudden and unexpected manner, like an accident. In that case, the shock compounds the loss, making it even more difficult to cope.

But a loss of our abilities does not make us less of a reflection of God. We're still an adored child of God, created in his image. Know that God comforts those suffering loss. And when the unseen wounds of loss heal over, we are better able to comfort others who suffer.

DAY 257

"The LORD is slow to anger but great in power; the LORD will not leave the guilty unpunished. His way is in the whirlwind and the storm, and clouds are the dust of his feet."

—NAHUM 1:3

God has an infinite amount of power. That idea might bring to mind a Zeus-like character sitting on a cloud, tossing angry lightning bolts down at mere mortals like us. But that's not God's heart at all. He has all the power in the world, yes, but he also has all the patience in the world. He doesn't zap every person who does him wrong—thankfully for us, since we would all be included in that category.

We should seek to reflect this excellent balance of God's character. We aren't as powerful as God, and we don't have the ability to throw lightning bolts. But harsh, angry words sure can feel like flaming arrows when we shoot them at others. We should be extra careful with the power we wield—the power of our words and actions. In practicing the sort of patience we see from God, we can avoid causing hurt in others. Being slow to anger helps us properly use the power God has granted to his creations.

DAY 258

"Because they all saw him and were terrified. Immediately he spoke to them and said, 'Take courage! It is I. Don't be afraid.'"

—MARK 6:50

Have you ever noticed when reading the Bible how most people's default response to God and angels is fear? And in this verse from Mark, we see Jesus's own disciples terrified by him as he walks toward them on the water.

Displays of God's supernatural power can be scary. He's an awfully big God, and we're awfully tiny humans. But as Jesus said to his closest friends here, we don't need to be afraid. We should respect God and his great power, but we don't need to be terrified of him. Like all aspects of God's character, his power bends our knees in humble, appropriate worship—think of all the things our God can do! But the sort of fear that leaves us shaking, doubting, and struck with terror doesn't need to have a place in our hearts. Take courage!

DAY 259

"This third I will put into the fire; I will refine them like silver and test them like gold. They will call on my name and I will answer them; I will say, 'They are my people,' and they will say, 'The Lord is our God.'"

—ZECHARIAH 13:9

We recognize that God is great and powerful and that he can always act, as long as the action is in accordance with the rest of his character. But what about those times God *could* act . . . and he chooses not to?

Ouch. Those times can be some of the more painful moments in our lives. Those are the moments that can leave us questioning God's will. If he *could* act to spare us from suffering, why wouldn't he? Doesn't he love us?

These are tough, tough questions. Sometimes hindsight offers us perspective. Once we're on the other side of the suffering, it may become clear why God brought us through that fire instead of around it. Other times, we don't get the "why" and we'll have to wait until we see God face-to-face to find our answers. But one thing we do know is that God doesn't waste our suffering. He uses the toughest experiences of our lives to refine us. We learn perseverance, patience, and empathy through our hard times. And by God's own power, we are held up—sustained until the day we are delivered from our suffering.

DAY 260

"Stop drinking only water, and use a little wine because of your stomach and your frequent illnesses."
—1 TIMOTHY 5:23

Poor Timothy. Apparently he had issues with his stomach *and* other frequent illnesses. If you suffer from any sort of chronic medical condition, then you can certainly relate. Chronic suffering can interfere with our daily lives as well as our emotional health.

It's important that we don't allow the effects of chronic suffering to give us the wrong idea about God. That's why this little personal note from Paul in his letter to Timothy is so cool. While it may seem like a mundane, unimportant memo—and probably isn't sound medical advice for our modern era—it tells us something that could serve as a crucial lifeline when we're dealing with suffering, especially the chronic kind.

When we suffer and God does not intervene for us, it does not mean we lack faith. Timothy was a man of great faith—one of Paul's protégés who went on to become a great leader in his own right. If even Timothy suffered in this way, we can take heart that chronic suffering doesn't simply affect those who lack the faith to be healed. If it can happen to Timothy, it can happen to us.

DAY 261

"His disciples asked him, 'Rabbi, who sinned, this man or his parents, that he was born blind?' 'Neither this man nor his parents sinned,' said Jesus, 'but this happened so that the works of God might be displayed in him.'"

—JOHN 9:2–3

In Jesus's time, it was assumed that if someone was suffering, it was because of that person's sin or the sin of his parents. So on top of dealing with the very difficult reality of being a disabled person in Ancient Judea, you'd have to deal with the public judgment that your disability came from sin in you or your family. Ugh.

Thankfully, this view isn't quite as common in our modern society. But perhaps when we're suffering, we wonder privately—what did I do to deserve this? Is God punishing me? Does God love me less than my friend who isn't suffering?

Those kinds of questions pierce our hearts. And that's why Jesus's words here are so deeply important. He says neither the blind man nor his parents sinned. This particular suffering occurred simply because it was part of God's big-picture plan for Jesus to be able to heal this man. God always has reasons why he allows suffering. Even if we don't get those reasons in this life, we can rest assured that suffering isn't automatically a result of our sin.

"Now I rejoice in what I am suffering for you, and I fill up in my flesh what is still lacking in regard to Christ's afflictions, for the sake of his body, which is the church."

—COLOSSIANS 1:24

When we suffer, it's easy to feel like we're alone. But that's definitely not the truth. We're never alone in our suffering. In fact, there is a fellowship of suffering in the world. It's like the Fellowship of the Ring, but with fewer hobbits. (Though our trials may feel like orcs sometimes . . .)

While we probably don't (and shouldn't!) wish suffering on anyone else, it's comforting to know we're not alone when we experience troubles. That's why support groups for various hardships are so common. When a group of people is afflicted with the same problem, they can band together for support and strength.

Even if you don't know anyone who is going through the exact same thing you're going through at the precise moment you're experiencing it, you're still not alone. The Holy Spirit is always close to you, within you, there to comfort, strengthen, and encourage you through the darkest tunnels.

DAY 263

"If we are thrown into the blazing furnace, the God we serve is able to deliver us from it, and he will deliver us from Your Majesty's hand. But even if he does not, we want you to know, Your Majesty, that we will not serve your gods or worship the image of gold you have set up."

—DANIEL 3:17–18

This is one of the coolest stories in the Bible. Shadrach, Meshach, and Abednego are making the brave choice to stand up to King Nebuchadnezzar when he tries to force them to worship an idol of gold. If you know the story, you know the king throws them into the furnace as punishment, but they are miraculously saved.

But one of the coolest parts of this story comes before the big miracle. It's this line: *but even if he does not.* These three righteous Israelites told the king that their God was able to save them from the fire. *But even if God chose not to save them,* they still would not bow down to the idol. That's because they knew it might better serve God's purposes not to save them. Their faith in God and their commitment to him was not contingent upon God choosing to rescue them from their suffering. Wow.

What a powerful example of faith for us! God may choose not to rescue us but he's still God—righteous, good, holy, and powerful. And for those reasons, we worship him willingly.

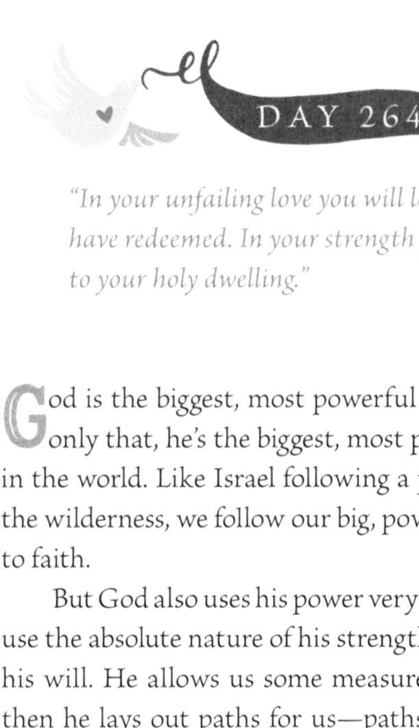

DAY 264

"In your unfailing love you will lead the people you have redeemed. In your strength you will guide them to your holy dwelling."

—EXODUS 15:13

God is the biggest, most powerful force in our lives. Not only that, he's the biggest, most powerful force for good in the world. Like Israel following a pillar of cloud through the wilderness, we follow our big, powerful God on the path to faith.

But God also uses his power very specifically. He doesn't use the absolute nature of his strength to force us to bend to his will. He allows us some measure of our own will, and then he lays out paths for us—paths to salvation, paths to faith, paths to righteousness, paths to growth. He leads and inspires and lights sparks inside us, but he doesn't force us. It's a curious balance—one that theologians have been arguing about for millennia (don't even get them started!).

When we see that God not only possesses great power but he uses it in such a way that he allows us to be involved in our process of faith, it becomes even clearer that it is right and good to have God rule our lives. What more excellent leader could we ask for but a God who loves us so deeply?

DAY 265

"For you are a people holy to the LORD your God. The LORD your God has chosen you out of all the peoples on the face of the earth to be his people, his treasured possession."

—DEUTERONOMY 7:6

God chose *you*. As he chose Israel to be his people under the old covenant, so he has chosen his church under the new covenant of Jesus. Wow. That's an amazing, baffling, wonderful truth. He has chosen you because it was his will to do so. He has chosen you because he's able to. It's yet another outflowing of his power.

We know he doesn't choose any of us because of anything righteous in and of ourselves (Romans 9:16). He chooses us because it pleases him. Like everything tied to God's power, this ought to make us pause, step back, and let it soak in. God loved you so much, he selected you. And God is mighty enough to carry out this act of love. It's not simply a greeting-card sound bite to say you are adored. This is real and actual proof of it!

DAY 266

"For the grace of God has appeared that offers salvation to all people."

—TITUS 2:11

When we think of all the ways God's power is displayed, we could probably brainstorm a list of a hundred different things off the tops of our heads. Is creation his mightiest deed? Is it the fact that he chooses us to be his people? His countless miracles throughout history?

All of those are mighty works of his powerful hand. But perhaps the best display of God's power is the fact that he saves us. Humankind is in quite a spiritual mess. As descendants of Adam, our relationship with God is automatically out of whack. And as we grow older and make choices that are selfish or wrong, we can drive a larger and larger wedge between ourselves and God.

But God doesn't leave us there. He draws us close, allows us to see Jesus, and he pulls us into faith—back into right relationship with him. That he made a way for mankind to get out of its sin mess may be the greatest show of power from our omnipotent God.

DAY 267

"You stretch out your right hand, and the earth swallows your enemies."

—EXODUS 15:12

Have you ever been in a situation that seemed completely impossible, only to watch as a door suddenly opens or a light appears at the end of the tunnel?

Maybe some of those events can be explained naturally—this circumstance or that led to an improbable outcome. But oftentimes, there's no earthly reason why things worked out so well for us just when everything seemed bleak.

That's because God fights for us. He goes to bat for his people. He sees the impossible circumstances we face and says, "Not today." Then he intervenes on our behalf. And when you're delivered from that deep, dark place, it can feel like a tiny, personal parting of the Red Sea. The times God fights for us are special. Store up those supernatural interventions in your heart. They can serve as reminders to ourselves if we ever feel tempted to forget how powerful God is.

DAY 268

"For you know that it was not with perishable things such as silver or gold that you were redeemed from the empty way of life handed down to you from your ancestors, but with the precious blood of Christ, a lamb without blemish or defect. He was chosen before the creation of the world, but was revealed in these last times for your sake."

—1 PETER 1:18–20

The cross is such a curious thing. In all of God's strength, there is no limit to the ways he could have saved us. Salvation could have been as earth-moving as creation, if he'd wanted it to be. Salvation could have been loud, showy, huge—anything.

Yet he chose the cross. He chose to send Jesus to earth as a man, with all the limitations of humankind. Not only did Jesus come to earth as a man, he lived a sinless life, then died a horrific death on the cross. Of all the ways God might have engineered salvation, this was what he chose. Strange! But also wonderful.

In the cross, we see the depth and breadth of God's love. We see the perfect humility of Jesus in the fact that he obeyed his father's will to become a man and then die when he didn't deserve it. We have the perfect example to follow in Jesus's life. The cross may puzzle us—but we also know it was meant to teach us.

DAY 269

"So do not throw away your confidence; it will be richly rewarded. You need to persevere so that when you have done the will of God, you will receive what he has promised."

—HEBREWS 10:35–36

Waiting on God's timing can be hard. Really, really hard. When we want something, we generally want it now. Yesterday, even. But so often, God makes us wait. Argh! Why?!

When we think about how mighty God is, perhaps it becomes a little easier to trust in his timing. Because God is all-powerful, he *could* act at any moment. Nothing is hindering God acting as he pleases. The fact that he may choose not to act in a given situation tells us something important. It tells us that, for whatever reason, it is of greater benefit for God to act at a different time.

Perhaps there's a piece of the puzzle we can't see yet (there usually is). Perhaps there is greater character growth for us if we discipline ourselves by waiting. Whatever the reason, we know God can act, so when he chooses not to, there is a reason. Let that truth bring you peace when you're waiting!

DAY 270

"'On the day when I act,' says the LORD Almighty, 'they will be my treasured possession. I will spare them, just as a father has compassion and spares his son who serves him.'"

—MALACHI 3:17

It's truly marvelous how God's attributes—all the wonderful traits that make up who he has revealed himself to be—intersect with one another. Not only is it marvelous, sometimes it's wild.

If we think of God's power, a huge zap of lightning and crack of thunder might come to mind. Or a ground-splitting earthquake. Or a flood of biblical proportions. Indeed, these things are sometimes referred to as "acts of God." But this verse outlines an intersection of God's traits that paint us a different picture of his power.

Here, it says on the day God *acts*—in other words, the day he shows his power—he will show his adored people compassion. Instead of acting in a massive display of destruction, God's action in this case is a great display of love and mercy. We don't only serve a great, powerful God. We also serve a God who is a gentle, loving Father.

DAY 271

"But the LORD is the true God; he is the living God, the eternal King."

—JEREMIAH 10:10A

The *true God* . . . what does that mean? It means God is the true God over all other "gods"—including things like money or success that we sometimes put before our faith. It also means that God himself is true. His words and promises to you will never fade or change. He'll never flip-flop on an issue or mislead you. He'll never lie or change his mind. This kind of absolute truth is unique to God—not even the best, most honest people we know tell the truth, the whole truth, and nothing but the truth all the time!

This attribute of God is wonderfully affirming for his adored children. It means our God is real, faithful, reliable, and he lives up to his promises. He does not lie or change his mind. God *is* truth itself.

DAY 272

"Indeed, if you call out for insight and cry aloud for understanding, and if you look for it as for silver and search for it as for hidden treasure, then you will understand the fear of the Lord and find the knowledge of God."

—PROVERBS 2:3–5

Wouldn't it be great if we got to define what is true and what isn't? Whatever we felt in any given moment would be true. Whatever we decided was fact simply was. On second thought . . . that sounds pretty terrible. We'd be creating an ever-evolving idea of right and wrong, an ever-changing standard of good and bad. That creates a pretty strange, unstable view of reality.

And yet this is the direction that our society leans. Many people believe that truth is relative and we're free to define our own realities—that the way we feel or think about something is the highest standard of truth.

But that's not what the Bible says, and that's not what God affirms. The Bible says knowledge belongs to God. Truth belongs to God. *He* gets to define what is true and real and right. Rather than feel restricted by this, we should view it as a blessing. Truth is not dependent on our feelings in the moment. It depends on the unmovable God of love.

DAY 273

"I have no greater joy than to hear that my children are walking in the truth."

—3 JOHN 4

Feelings can be really powerful things. Opinions can be incredibly strong too. If you haven't witnessed the power of opinions, just listen to a conversation between two people on opposite ends of any political issue. Yikes!

And the thing about these strong, opposing opinions or feelings is that both people involved absolutely believe they're in the right. No question about it. But two totally opposing views can't both be right, can they? Generally not. So if the power of our feelings or the strength of our opinions aren't indicators of truth, what is?

It's simple, really. If our thinking lines up with God's thinking, then our thinking is true. We can look to God's Word to show us his heart on many issues. And it's vitally important that we work to line up our thinking with God's heart and not attempt to do the opposite—force God's Word to match our opinions.

"For I have always been mindful of your unfailing love and have lived in reliance on your faithfulness."

—PSALM 26:3

God's faithfulness is like a rock for us to stand on. What does it mean to be faithful? It means steadfast in allegiance (loyal) and firmly holding to one's promises. God embodies both of these things. His faithfulness is one facet of his truthfulness. In other words, if he says he's going to remain beside us, he will. If he says he loves us, he does. If he says you're an adored daughter of his, you are.

God's faithfulness means he follows through on everything he says he will. It means that if he says something will come to pass, it will. We should seek to mirror God's faithfulness in our lives too. We should be people of our word. If we say we're going to do something, we need to follow through. We should show loyalty, first and foremost to God, himself. Seek to be a faithful follower—of God's Word and your own.

DAY 275

"Now faith is confidence in what we hope for and assurance about what we do not see."

—HEBREWS 11:1

The heart of faith is taking God at his word. As the writer of Hebrews says, faith is being assured of what we can't see. In our modern society, where everything must be proven by the scientific method, how can anyone possibly be assured of something they can't see? So assured, in fact, that they're willing to build their entire life around that assurance?

It may sound crazy to some. But to God's children, it makes perfect sense. We have faith in God because we believe he is who he says he is. That's the definition of faith—trusting in the truthfulness of God's declarations about himself, his son, and salvation. We believe God is telling the truth when he says what's right and what's wrong. We are assured of God's character and his promises. We have faith because first, God is faithful to his Word.

DAY 276

"Lord, who may dwell in your sacred tent? Who may live on your holy mountain? The one whose walk is blameless, who does what is righteous, who speaks the truth from their heart."

—PSALM 15:1–2

Some of the things the Bible tells us to *avoid* are physical, external actions—idolatry, debauchery, or drunkenness, for example. Some of the things we're told to *practice* are physical, external actions—care for widows and orphans, generosity, or speaking out on behalf of the overlooked. But many other things we're told to be aware of are heart issues—sins or virtues that are tucked deep inside our hearts in places that only God can see all the time.

Truthfulness and faithfulness are heart issues. They are secret virtues God can see. But even those things hidden deep within our hearts tend to spill out—usually from our mouths. Here, the psalmist says those who may dwell in God's sacred tent are the ones who speak truth from their hearts. Heart issues matter to God as much as external actions. We need to be mindful of what's going on beneath the surface of our lives. If we have external acts of generosity but hearts and mouths full of untruth, we're not going to be living the fullest relationships we could—with others or with God.

DAY 277

"Know therefore that the Lord *your God is God; he is the faithful God, keeping his covenant of love to a thousand generations of those who love him and keep his commandments."*

—DEUTERONOMY 7:9

God's reliability is a big part of who he is. He does what he says he'll do, when he says he'll do it. We see this countless times throughout Scripture, in both the Old and New Testaments. You've probably even witnessed God's reliability in your own life. Maybe he has answered a prayer, given you wisdom through his Word, or simply provided comfort during a hard time. Those are all examples of God's reliability.

God is dependable. His words mean something. When he says he'll do something, he will. We should seek to reflect this godly trait in our lives. There isn't much in our world we can depend upon these days. At any time, we might be surrounded by political, social, or economic upheaval. Let's seek to be a safe spot in the chaos for others the way God is a safe spot in the chaos for us.

"Do not lie to each other, since you have taken off your old self with its practices and have put on the new self, which is being renewed in knowledge in the image of its Creator."

—COLOSSIANS 3:9–10

We never need to fear the search for knowledge and truth. Sometimes people think those things are mutually exclusive with faith. But the opposite is true! God's truthfulness means he is truth and knowledge itself. When we thirst for such things, we are simply discovering the truth God already knows.

Our sparks of curiosity surrounding science, social studies (world cultures, history, geography), and humanities (philosophy, religion, literature, art, music) are good, God-given traits. Feed your hunger in those areas! Our minds are being renewed by God's truth and knowledge, and so our discernment will protect us from the world's faulty reasoning. Intellectual curiosity can help give us a deep, robust faith that always has a ready answer for those who are still searching for God's ultimate truth in their lives.

DAY 279

"Keep your mouth free of perversity; keep corrupt talk far from your lips."

—PROVERBS 4:24

We live in an age obsessed with sensationalism. Fake news, click-bait articles, and heavily biased media outlets litter the Internet. The value of truth seems to cheapen by the minute. So what can we, God's daughters, do about it? How can we uphold a high standard of truth when so many around us seem not to care?

One practical action we can take is to make sure anything we share on social media is fact-checked. Find the least-biased news sources and support those outlets with your clicks. Avoid the splashy, sensational headlines with little real value to the articles. Same thing goes for talking with friends or writing papers for class. Don't spread information that you can't back up, whether that's shady news stories or rumors about your classmates.

The truth matters to God, so it should matter to us. Let's do our part to keep biased, untrue, or gossipy news far from our lives.

DAY 280

"Sanctify them by the truth; your word is truth."

—JOHN 17:17

John says we are *sanctified* by God's truth. But what does that mean, exactly? Sanctification in the New Testament is a spiritual process where the Holy Spirit helps us to grow in Christlikeness. Which is just a fancy way to say our minds, hearts, and desires become more and more like Jesus's mind, heart, and desires.

God's truth plays a very active role in that sanctification process for us. Our study of God's Word helps us to cleanse displeasing things from our lives and hearts—bad habits, little pockets of sin we're trying to hold onto, meanness or selfishness. It helps us to strive toward the things we know God wants us to do—being kind to others, valuing the truth, helping those in need. And God's Word helps us to put on God's mind, so to speak. We read about the things God cares about. We begin to allow his view of others to become our view of others. Putting on the mind of God helps us love better. God's words are truth, itself, and they have a real, spiritual effect on our hearts.

DAY 281

"Kings take pleasure in honest lips; they value the one who speaks what is right."

—PROVERBS 16:13

Truth doesn't just matter in our spiritual lives. It's something that is vitally important to authority figures who oversee us. At various stages of our lives, those authority figures may be our parents, our teachers, our bosses, or our governments. Or even our coaches and mentors.

Like the kings mentioned in Proverbs, these authority figures should value honesty in the people they oversee. Our parents and bosses want to know they can trust us. They want to know our word is sound—that we're reliable, faithful, and honest.

Being trustworthy, honest, and faithful draws positive attention to your faith in Jesus. If you're known as the resident backstabber around school or the one who lies on her timecard at work, and then you start inviting people to church, it doesn't speak well of your faith. Or your savior. On the other hand, holding to the highest standards of honesty gives you a great platform to share your faith with others.

"Therefore each of you must put off falsehood and speak truthfully to your neighbor, for we are all members of one body."

—EPHESIANS 4:25

Truthfulness isn't optional, according to Scripture. It isn't one of those gray areas of freedom we have to navigate with care and responsibility. Truthfulness is commanded.

The truth is really important, but we should also handle the truth wisely. For example, we can be truthful without being brutally honest. If your best friend hates her new haircut, you don't need to affirm the brutal truth—that it makes her head look like a pumpkin. You also don't need to lie and tell her it looks awesome. But you can offer to help her learn how to style it. Or even go hat shopping.

Being truthful also doesn't mean you should spill all the secrets you've been entrusted with. That's gossiping, not truthfulness. But it *is* okay to tell a secret if you know someone is in trouble or doing something dangerous. Be wise about your use of the truth!

DAY 283

"Rather, we have renounced secret and shameful ways; we do not use deception, nor do we distort the word of God. On the contrary, by setting forth the truth plainly we commend ourselves to everyone's conscience in the sight of God."

—2 CORINTHIANS 4:2

Have you ever heard the phrase "the end justifies the means"? Basically, it means that it doesn't matter how you get to the goal you want as long as you get there. Winning at all costs. Lying, cheating, and stealing one's way to the top. Or simply stepping on people to reach your goals.

This attitude is clearly *not* one that is acceptable by God's standards. Maybe that should go without saying. But in a world that tells you to ask forgiveness instead of permission, it's easy to compromise little bit by little bit until you're willing to do things that are clearly wrong if it helps you get where you'd like to go.

We need to have higher standards than that. We need to avoid secret and shameful ways that rely on deception or even twisting the Bible to justify what we want. Live in a way that sets the truth forth plainly and allows you to live with a clean conscience before God.

DAY 284

"You belong to your father, the devil, and you want to carry out your father's desires. He was a murderer from the beginning, not holding to the truth, for there is no truth in him. When he lies, he speaks his native language, for he is a liar and the father of lies."

—JOHN 8:44

Yikes. These are some harsh words spoken by Jesus. It's safe to say that Jesus has some strong feelings about lying—and, by extension, liars. Not only that, we can see that Satan delights in lies. Jesus even says lying is Satan's native language.

Sometimes it's tempting to insist that Satan is involved in every struggle we have. Have you ever heard the phrase "The devil made me do it?" It's a convenient place to place blame, but it's not very realistic. We struggle enough with our own hearts and our own human nature that oftentimes Satan doesn't even factor into the battle. But when it comes to lying, it's not an exaggeration to say Satan delights in lies.

It's safe to say that lying is something we should absolutely avoid. Lying is abhorrent to God and is something Jesus spoke strongly against too. Let's keep ourselves clean from the things God despises!

DAY 285

"Whoever conceals their sins does not prosper, but the one who confesses and renounces them finds mercy."

—PROVERBS 28:13

Have you ever been in a situation when you knew you could lie and get away with it? No one would ever know, so it wouldn't damage your relationships. No one could possibly get hurt, so what's the big deal . . . right?

The truth is, there are situations when a lie doesn't have much external consequence. But that doesn't mean it's a not a big deal. Getting away with a lie does not negate the spiritual consequences of that lie. Since lying is something God hates, telling lies will drive a wedge in your relationship with God. Whether you get caught or not.

Our true character is revealed in how we behave when we know we won't get caught. So let's strive to always act as if someone is watching us. Because, as we know, God is.

DAY 286

"How precious to me are your thoughts, God! How vast is the sum of them!"

—PSALM 139:17

Since God embodies truth itself, we may feel like we can't possibly reflect this trait. We'll always fall short! How can we ever measure up to God's standard of truthfulness?

Like all of God's traits, we can't exercise truthfulness perfectly the way God does. But we *can* reflect God's truthfulness. Not only should we strive for honesty in our lives, but we should study God's Word hard. When we spend time with Scripture, we begin to see the world the way God sees it. We begin to understand truth as God defines it.

While we may never be able to express any of God's characteristics perfectly, we want to be able to exclaim with the psalmist, "How precious to me are your thoughts, God!"

DAY 287

"Not one of all the LORD's good promises to Israel failed; every one was fulfilled."

—JOSHUA 21:45

God doesn't lie. And he doesn't fail. So when he promises something to his people, he makes good on that promise.

Scripture is full of the promises of God. Some were spoken specifically to Israel; some were spoken specifically to Jesus's followers. Others are for all people who have loved God throughout history and for those who will love God in the future. We can rest assured that whenever God speaks a promise, he will keep his word.

Do you know many of God's promises off the top of your head? If you've never looked into it before, you can search on your Bible app, look in the index of your study Bible, or even just read the next few devotions in this book to take a look at some of the many wonderful things God has in store.

DAY 288

"And this is what he promised us—eternal life."

—1 JOHN 2:25

One of God's greatest promises is eternal life. Eternal life is the ultimate completion of our relationship with God through Jesus. It is the ultimate triumph over sin and death that God ordained since the beginning of time. It doesn't get any more awesome than that!

Eternal life is an important part of our salvation story, but it's also something that applies to our daily lives. What? Eternal life matters in our day-to-day? How can that be? But it's true. God's promise of eternal life—and the fact that we *know* he will make good on that promise—gives us hope, strength, and endurance when facing hard times in our lives.

We have a very bright future promised to us. One without suffering, death, or pain. One without the sins of others and the sins of ourselves. When we're hurt, beaten down, and just plain tired of life on this imperfect planet, God's promise of that beautiful future can be our lifeline.

"No temptation has overtaken you except what is common to mankind. And God is faithful; he will not let you be tempted beyond what you can bear. But when you are tempted, he will also provide a way out so that you can endure it."

—1 CORINTHIANS 10:13

This is one of the very best promises in the New Testament. Seriously. First, Paul points out that we're not alone when we face temptation. In fact, Jesus himself was tempted in the worst ways possible. We never have to feel like no one else understands what it's like to be tempted with whatever we're facing.

Second, we will never be tempted beyond what we can bear. In other words, any temptation God allows us to face will never be irresistible. We have the strength in the Holy Spirit to resist that sin, whatever it is.

But perhaps most importantly, God will always provide a way out for us. Not only are we expected to rely on our strength and the strength of the Holy Spirit, but God himself provides a way for us to flee from that sin. Like an escape hatch to holiness. Remember that God has promised this to us when you feel pressed down by temptation. Look for God's escape hatch!

DAY 290

"Though I walk in the midst of trouble, you preserve my life. You stretch out your hand against the anger of my foes; with your right hand you save me."

—PSALM 138:7

Wouldn't it be nice if God promised we would have no troubles in this life? That, because we're his adored children, we get to move through life easily and without a care? We do get to look forward to something like that in eternity, but as far as this life goes, trouble-free isn't exactly on the agenda.

But God promises to walk beside us in our troubles. That doesn't mean he promises to deliver us from all those troubles. Sometimes we're saved from them; sometimes we're not. But we do have the unshakable promise that God will not leave us while we endure. He will preserve and sustain us as we handle trials with grace and faith.

When you're facing tough times, remember this promise. God has not abandoned you, and he never will.

DAY 291

"Peace I leave with you; my peace I give you. I do not give to you as the world gives. Do not let your hearts be troubled and do not be afraid."

—JOHN 14:27

The world can be a dark, scary place for anyone. Just turn on the evening news for ten minutes and you're bound to hear about something frightening—crime, wars, disease, accidents, illness. There's no shortage of it.

Yet another of God's great promises is that he will give us peace. The world and the enemy want to bring us fear. They want our fear to immobilize us so that we don't grow in faith, so that we fail to serve others, and so that the Kingdom of God is stopped in its tracks. But God says, nah, not today. He offers us supernatural peace—deliverance from our worries.

We may still struggle to overcome anxiety, doubts, and fear. It's difficult to perfectly lean on all of God's good promises in this life, and we each have areas where we struggle. But his peace is available, offered to us as an irrevocable promise.

DAY 292

"'Look, he is coming with the clouds,' and 'every eye will see him, even those who pierced him'; and all peoples on earth 'will mourn because of him.' So shall it be! Amen."

—REVELATION 1:7

Sometimes it's easy to feel like all that "last days" business doesn't have much to do with our lives. So we lump all those end-timey things together—heaven, eternity, resurrection, the second coming, the rapture—and stick it all in a box. And for a lot of people, that box has a giant question mark on it.

But each of these afterlife-related concerns *can* have an application to our daily lives, like we've seen with God's promise of eternity. Another of God's excellent promises for the future is the promise that Jesus will return to earth. Jesus's return is the catalyst that will usher in the rest of eternity.

Knowing that Jesus's second coming is imminent, we can remind ourselves that judgment belongs to God. And when we feel like the sin of the world is overwhelming, we can find peace in the knowledge that Jesus is coming soon. The troubles of this world won't last forever. That's reason to rejoice!

DAY 293

"For the Lord himself will come down from heaven, with a loud command, with the voice of the archangel and with the trumpet call of God, and the dead in Christ will rise first. After that, we who are still alive and are left will be caught up together with them in the clouds to meet the Lord in the air. And so we will be with the Lord forever."

—1 THESSALONIANS 4:16–17

Another of God's promises tucked into the end-timey box is the idea of resurrection. We understand that Jesus's resurrection happened two thousand years ago, but how often do we think about our own resurrection? When we think of the afterlife, we tend to focus on heaven. But heaven is only the beginning of eternity.

After Jesus returns to earth, the dead will be raised to life. Whoa! Not only that, the earth is going to be created anew. This is a wonderful promise. It is a promise to reverse all the damage that sin has done to God's original design. As resurrected humans will not get sick or die. The earth will not be in a slow state of decay. God's glorious creation will be restored to the glory he gave to it in the beginning—and that includes us! What hope we have for our future.

DAY 294

"'He will wipe every tear from their eyes. There will be no more death' or mourning or crying or pain, for the old order of things has passed away."

—REVELATION 21:4

It's sort of difficult to imagine life without pain. There are lots of different types of pain—physical, emotional, even spiritual. And people experience it to varying degrees. Some have very difficult paths to travel in their lives while others hit relatively few potholes along the way. But one thing is sure—every human being will experience pain and suffering to some degree in her lifetime. It's a given.

So how amazing is it that God promises us a future without pain? That's part of the resurrection body and new earth promise. In a new creation, one that's free of sin, we never have to experience sadness or heartache. We won't suffer tragedy or loss. There won't be pain—at all!

That's a glorious promise. When we trudge through the hardships of this life, we can always keep our painless future full of worshiping God in sight. No matter how difficult things get here and now, that's what we have on the horizon. Hallelujah!

DAY 295

"Our God is in heaven; he does whatever pleases him."

—PSALM 115:3

God is perfectly free—free to carry out his entire will without anything or anyone hindering him. God's power and his freedom work together to bring about his will so that he keeps his truthful promises. Isn't it cool how all God's attributes work together to make our great God who he is?

God's freedom means we never have to be afraid that God will be thwarted. We don't have to worry that God wishes something would happen but can't bring it about—that someone will be able to stop what God wants to happen. God has plans for the world, for the church, and for each of our lives. He is free and able to make these things happen. When we desperately wish something would happen for us and we pray about it, but it doesn't come to pass, we don't need to worry that perhaps something stopped God from carrying out his will. Instead, we know God has a bigger, better plan for us—and that he's working on making it happen!

DAY 296

"So do not fear, for I am with you; do not be dismayed, for I am your God. I will strengthen you and help you; I will uphold you with my righteous right hand."

—ISAIAH 41:10

Have you ever been in a situation that made you anxious, concerned, or downright terrified? We experience fear over all sorts of things, from a big exam in a tough class, to passing your driver's license test, to writing an essay for a college application. Or maybe you're facing a huge, scary life change—like your parents' divorce or the death of someone close to you.

Whatever the scale, we have all felt fear many times. And when we face the really tough, scary stuff, we may ask ourselves why God doesn't intervene. It can definitely feel confusing. If God is always free to act, then why doesn't he? But our understanding of God's freedom can actually bring peace to our hearts in difficult times. Sometimes he lets us face the scary moments so we can grow. Sometimes he does it because he sees the big picture, and this difficult experience is going to help us or someone else in the future.

When God is free to act, but chooses not to, we can have peace in the assurance that whatever trouble we're currently experiencing, it is in some way working for our good.

DAY 297

"[God], will you never look away from me, or let me alone even for an instant? If I have sinned, what have I done to you, you who see everything we do? Why have you made me your target? Have I become a burden to you?"

—JOB 7:19–20

Sometimes we have a perfect, pretty picture of what faith looks like. The wide-eyed, unquestioning acceptance of everything that happens to us. The flawless peace, patience, joy, and wisdom that rolls off the faithful in waves so real, you can practically see them. The heart that never questions, never doubts, and always remains steady, no matter the pain or difficulty we experience.

Does that sound like you? Me neither. But that doesn't mean our faith is less real. The truth is, it's okay to ask *why*. Think of how many psalms find the author crying out to God, begging for intervention. Or how often Job asked why he was experiencing such hardship. *Why* is okay. Wrestling with our faith is okay—as long as we keep it in perspective.

Job asked why, but he learned quickly that God does not answer to anyone but himself. When God finally spoke, he pointed out that he is God, who gives and takes away, and Job needed to keep that in perspective. God's heart is near to us when we're suffering. But we must remember to stay humble in respect of God's freedom and his power.

DAY 298

"A new command I give you: Love one another. As I have loved you, so you must love one another."

—JOHN 13:34

God is always free to do whatever he wants. If he wanted to, he could turn the world upside down. He could destroy the earth or bring time to an end. He could usher in another ice age or another flood. If he wanted to, he could make mankind go the way of the dinosaur.

But with all the things he could do—many of them terrifying—God chooses love. He chose to redeem human beings and give us a way back to him—a way to escape from sin and death. He chose to love us to the point of the cross.

And that's why love matters so much to God. He chose love above death and destruction, and he calls his children to choose love above hate, love above death.

DAY 299

"For the LORD has chosen Jacob to be his own, Israel to be his treasured possession."

—PSALM 135:4

Our free God chooses love, and he also chooses people. He always has. Just as he chose Jacob (the Israelite people) in the days of the Old Testament, he has chosen his church in this age. And that means you.

Have you ever thought about that before? Out of all the things God is free to do, he chose to adore us. He chose to adore *you*—just as you are. He chose you before you even knew who he was. It's pretty incredible to let those truths sink in. A God whose freedom is so ingrained as to be part of his character chooses us for his church.

Let that truth inspire you to serve others today. How can you help the world see the love God has for them too?

"The thief comes only to steal and kill and destroy; I have come that they may have life, and have it to the full."

—JOHN 10:10

We don't have the level of freedom God has. Can you imagine being able to carry out your entire will all the time? Free lattes and warm chocolate-chip cookies for all!

But while we don't have God's level of freedom, we do get some freedom in our lives—and it's a huge blessing to live lives "to the full" in this freedom. Our freedom comes in the form of being able to choose when and how to act, speak, and think. We're free to have opinions and to make choices. We're free to have our own identities.

For some, circumstances have robbed them of these human freedoms. Sometimes accident, illness, or injury take away physical or mental ability and restrict our freedom. Some of us were born with such restrictions. Others have their freedom of speech or choice taken away by a restrictive government. Sometimes being born into a tough economic situation limits our choices.

Make an effort to appreciate the freedoms you have. They are a gift from God, a reflection of his own free nature.

DAY 301

"But you are a chosen people, a royal priesthood, a holy nation, God's special possession, that you may declare the praises of him who called you out of darkness into his wonderful light."

—1 PETER 2:9

People have human freedom to varying degrees, depending on their circumstances. But there's a special kind of freedom that Christians experience because our sins have been covered by Jesus's sacrifice on the cross. Our debt to God has been paid, so we no longer live in fear of condemnation. And with the payment of that debt comes freedom.

But it's incredibly important that we don't misuse this freedom. Christians are not saved so that we have the freedom to keep on sinning. We are saved to become a "royal priesthood." We're saved to build God's kingdom and to praise him—both in our words and our actions.

The best use of our Christian freedom is to allow God's Spirit to share the love of Jesus with others, free from fear.

DAY 302

"You, my brothers and sisters, were called to be free. But do not use your freedom to indulge the flesh; rather, serve one another humbly in love."

—GALATIANS 5:13

Perhaps you're blessed to live in a nation that grants you lots of freedom and rights. The Constitution of the United States grants its citizens many freedoms, like freedom of religion, speech, freedom of press, the right to bear arms, protection against unlawful "search and seizure," just to name a few.

U.S. citizens also have the right to vote for their representative government. When you think about the whole of history, this is an amazing amount of freedom for the "common" person to hold. Kids who are U.S. citizens also have the right to a free public education. That's an amazing blessing!

It's important we use our political freedom and rights responsibly. That means being an informed voter and maintaining an awareness of our history and our current events. It means using our freedom to bring about good, both in our country and in the world. It also means making the most of that free education—even if we'd rather be binge-watching something on Netflix than doing homework.

DAY 303

"His divine power has given us everything we need for a godly life through our knowledge of him who called us by his own glory and goodness. Through these he has given us his very great and precious promises, so that through them you may participate in the divine nature, having escaped the corruption in the world caused by evil desires."

—2 PETER 1:3–4

We can think of freedom in big, spiritual terms (our Christian freedom) and in big, social terms (our political freedom). We also have a much smaller, more daily freedom, but it's just as important as our "big freedoms."

We have the freedom to choose how we will treat other people. We have the freedom to choose kind words or sharp words. We have the freedom to choose actions that glorify God or dishonor him. We are free to choose to love others or to curse them. We are free to choose selfish deeds or deeds that serve others.

These "little" freedoms aren't little at all. And how we use them says a lot about us. Let's let our use of small, daily freedoms to act as we choose shine the light of God bright in a dark world that needs it.

DAY 304

"They will do no wrong; they will tell no lies. A deceitful tongue will not be found in their mouths. They will eat and lie down and no one will make them afraid."

—ZEPHANIAH 3:13

Remember that Spider-Man quote that has its roots in Luke 12:48? "With great power comes great responsibility." We could just as easily say "With great freedom comes great responsibility."

Sometimes we misunderstand freedom of speech to mean we can say whatever we want, whenever we want, without consequence. If you've ever back-talked your parents or a teacher, you know this isn't true. You certainly *can* say those things, but you will also certainly reap the consequences.

Our freedom in other areas is similar. Freedom is a great gift, but with it comes the responsibility of dealing with the consequences when we exercise those freedoms in ways that are unwise. If we're rude or unkind to our parents, we may be punished. If we're disrespectful to our bosses, we might be fired. If we speak harsh, careless words to a friend, we might lose that friendship. If we behave foolishly, we may damage our reputations and lose the respect of those around us. Show how deeply you value your freedom by using it wisely!

"Continue to remember those in prison as if you were together with them in prison, and those who are mistreated as if you yourselves were suffering."

—HEBREWS 13:3

If you live in a free society, you've probably witnessed your fellow citizens having heated discussions about the finer points of our freedoms. How to interpret certain parts of the Constitution or which leaders deserve to be elected to certain positions or how to apply laws written hundreds of years ago to our modern society.

It's easy to get caught up in it and forget that we are deeply blessed even to be able to have these debates. Many across the world don't enjoy free governments. Some don't have freedom of religion and find themselves on the wrong side of the law simply because they are followers of Jesus. Others live in areas ripped apart by war and are unable to experience simple freedoms we take for granted.

As the writer of Hebrews encourages his readers, remember those in prison—whether that's a literal prison or those who are "imprisoned" by oppressive governments, wars, or famines. Remembering those who don't enjoy the level of freedom you do will inspire you to actively pray for the suffering people around the world, as well as uncover a deeper appreciation for the freedoms you have.

DAY 306

"Be very careful, then, how you live—not as unwise but as wise, making the most of every opportunity, because the days are evil. Therefore do not be foolish, but understand what the Lord's will is."

—EPHESIANS 5:15–17

God may exist outside of time—but we don't. Time is a very important factor in our lives, whether we like it or not. If you're the type who loves calendars and schedules and plans, maybe time simply feels like the perfect, neat segments on your color-coded day planner. (Not judging.) Or maybe you're the type who just felt slightly queasy reading that. (Also not judging.)

Either way, time management skills are an excellent skillset to develop. Time is a limited resource, and God wants us to use all of our resources in effective and efficient ways. As Paul writes here, we should make the most of every opportunity—both to discern God's will for our lives, as the verse discusses, but also in the daily matter of managing our time.

You never have to love planners and calendars if you're not built that way. But are there other ways you can help yourself be more productive throughout your day? Lists, prioritizing tasks, and rewarding yourself for meeting small goals are all effective ways to help increase your productivity and becoming better at time management.

DAY 307

"As far as the east is from the west, so far has he removed our transgressions from us."

—PSALM 103:12

Have you ever felt like you failed God? Maybe a year ago, you felt like he adored and delighted in you. But now you feel like you've made some mistakes, so God couldn't possibly feel that way about you anymore.

Take heart. God's eternity means that our pasts and our futures are no surprise to God.

So that moment when you felt really close to God? He still sees that moment, clear as crystal as if it's happening now. The love he had for you then still stands now. He knew what mistakes you'd make a long time ago—two thousand years ago, in fact, as Jesus trudged to the cross. That's *why* Jesus went to the cross. He knew exactly how much we needed it. When we feel far from God, it's not because we've messed up so badly God has walked away from us. It's usually because we've walked away from God. But we always have the opportunity to turn away from our mistakes and do better tomorrow—to regain our closeness with the Lord.

DAY 308

"'I am the Alpha and the Omega,' says the Lord God, 'who is, and who was, and who is to come, the Almighty.'"

—REVELATION 1:8

Our world runs by the clock. We have our days, months, and years divided into handy segments by which we manage our schedules, our plans, our goals . . . even our dreams. We fantasize about reaching certain milestones in the future. And that all depends on time.

So it's pretty strange to think about God's eternity. God has no beginning and no end. It's not as though he's the first created being on a string of created things. He simply *always* has been. And not only did he create our entire world, he created time itself. Whoa. That's some crazy, heady business. But it's true. God has always been in existence, and he exists outside of time.

And even so, God reaches down to our level and responds to us in time, as our lives unfold. It's yet another example of how deeply he loves us—how thoroughly he's willing to meet us at our own level and in ways we can understand and relate to.

DAY 309

"Be still before the LORD and wait patiently for him; do not fret when people succeed in their ways, when they carry out their wicked schemes."

—PSALM 37:7

Waiting is tough. When we want something really badly, waiting can even be excruciating. Sometimes being told "not now" is worse than being told "no." "No" allows us to let it go and move on. "Not now" means we have to be patient and wait. Argh!

Why does God make us wait? Sometimes when we wait, we realize that thing we want isn't what we want at all. We realize we wanted quick gratification. Sometimes a little time is all we need to realize our wants aren't what's best for us. Sometimes God wants to help us build up our patience. Ever heard that "patience is a virtue"? It's true. It's listed as a fruit of the Spirit. Increased patience builds our character and makes us more like Jesus.

And perhaps most of all, God wants us to trust him. He wants us to lean on him completely. The more we trust his wisdom and his plan, the quicker we are to settle into the "not now" moments and believe that God has good things in store for us.

DAY 310

"But seek first his kingdom and his righteousness, and all these things will be given to you as well."

—MATTHEW 6:33

Waiting for anything, even the small things, is tough. But what about when we're told to wait for the greatest hopes and dreams of our lives? That's triple tough. It makes matters even more difficult when God doesn't give us a clear answer about our dreams. That silence can turn into "not now" or "not ever," and there's no way to tell the difference.

So what can we do? Turn your dreams over to God. That doesn't just mean surrendering the ultimate answer of whether or not you can achieve that dream to God, though that's part of it. It also means finding the balance between putting God's kingdom first and taking practical steps on the path toward your dream. God may tell us to wait. He may eventually redirect our dreams and give us new ones. When we put his kingdom first, we're more sensitive to these leadings.

Putting God before our dreams is difficult but worth it. It keeps our hearts humble and turned toward God so our dreams don't become idols in our lives.

DAY 311

"Why, you do not even know what will happen tomorrow. What is your life? You are a mist that appears for a little while and then vanishes."

—JAMES 4:14

Have you ever seen an advertisement for something in which the advertisers entice you to take immediate action with the word "limited time only"? It's a pretty effective strategy. We don't want to miss out on a good deal or a cool bonus by failing to respond quickly enough. Limited time only offers prod us into action so we don't lose our chance.

Our lives are limited time only too. No one knows exactly how much time she has on earth. But we all know our lives won't stretch on forever. Are you approaching your life—your plans, your relationships on earth, and your relationship with God—as if it's limited time only?

Considering our short time on earth should inspire us to make the most of our years—to love as much as possible, to work as hard as we can, to laugh and play and serve like it's going out of style. Tomorrow is not promised, so live your life and love God with the urgency of a "limited time only" offer.

DAY 312

"Perfume and incense bring joy to the heart, and the pleasantness of a friend springs from their heartfelt advice."

—PROVERBS 27:9

Time is a funny thing. It marches on at a steady pace, but it sure doesn't feel like it. Some days or weeks seem to stretch on for ages while others are over in a blink. But all time that passes leaves behind a trail of memories—some painful, others beautiful.

Beautiful memories should be treasured. Have you ever thought about keeping a memory box? Bits and pieces of the important moments of our lives can be powerful reminders of the many ways God has blessed us. Cards from friends, photos, ticket stubs, dried flowers from special events—the list of what could be included in such a box is endless. A memory box is like saving pieces of time from the seasons of our lives.

You don't have to keep your memories of good friends and excellent times in a literal box. Maybe a journal or a file folder or a digital library works better for you. Whatever method you prefer, think about remembering the special people in your life as time rolls on. You won't regret it!

DAY 313

"Do not gloat over me, my enemy! Though I have fallen, I will rise. Though I sit in darkness, the LORD will be my light."

—MICAH 7:8

The idea of the future can feel bright and exciting. Maybe when you think about the future, you're thrilled about the possibilities of going to college, getting married, having a career, having children, shooting for your dreams—or some combination of these things. Maybe you don't think about specifics but you're excited to see where God takes you.

But the future can also feel scary and uncertain. Wars, discrimination, natural disasters, and other terrible things fill the newspaper headlines. Sometimes it seems like the world is getting worse around us as we inch closer to Jesus's return to earth.

But we don't need to fear the future. Our eternal God has not only the world but each of our lives in his hands. While that doesn't mean we won't experience troubles in the future, it does mean that God is bringing about his ultimate plan as we speak. And he wants us to delight in all the cool opportunities he puts in our paths. Don't give in to fear of the uncertain world around us. Live fully in the time God has given to you!

DAY 314

"He said to me: 'It is done. I am the Alpha and the Omega, the Beginning and the End. To the thirsty I will give water without cost from the spring of the water of life.'"

—REVELATION 21:6

Sometimes we may look at our lives and wonder, in the face of eternity, how much we really matter. After all, each of us is only one small person—a daughter of God, sure, but still one tiny individual. So what impact could we possibly have that will last through eternity?

Honestly? Any individual can have a *huge* impact on eternity when she makes it her life's work to share the love of Jesus. Spreading Jesus's message impacts God's kingdom, and God's kingdom is eternal. Sharing Jesus's message of redemption can literally bring souls from death to life. There's nothing anyone can do that is more important than that.

We can build the kingdom in other ways that matter too. Helping others grow in their relationship with God is a big deal. The eternal impact that starts with you can fan out through anyone you help, support, love, teach, or inspire. Think of the hundreds or thousands—even millions—of people one small daughter of God can touch throughout her lifetime.

DAY 315

"Then the end will come, when he hands over the kingdom to God the Father after he has destroyed all dominion, authority and power. For he must reign until he has put all his enemies under his feet. The last enemy to be destroyed is death."

—1 CORINTHIANS 15:24–26

When Jesus ascended to heaven after the resurrection, he promised his disciples he would be returning to earth. The world as we know it will come to an end, and the final judgment will occur, ushering in a new era—what we sometimes refer to as "eternity," the rest of time.

It might seem strange when you hear Christians wishing Jesus would come soon. Doesn't that mean our lives are over? Time's up? No more chance at living? Yes, it does mean that in some ways. But when Christ returns to earth and the final judgment occurs, evil will be defeated once and for all. It might be the end of the type of lives that we know right now, but it's the start of a much better life—one free of sin and pain and suffering.

Even though we love and appreciate the lives we have now, we look forward to the future with hope and excitement. Jesus is coming back! That's something to celebrate.

DAY 316

"But you, dear friends, by building yourselves up in your most holy faith and praying in the Holy Spirit, keep yourselves in God's love as you wait for the mercy of our Lord Jesus Christ to bring you to eternal life."

—JUDE 20–21

When the future is overwhelming, it can be tough to stay on task. That's true when we're talking about our personal futures, and it's true when we're talking about the future of the world. When we're uncertain about tomorrow, how can we focus on today?

But no matter how unsure we feel of tomorrow—whether we're facing scary times politically, socially, or personally—the ultimate task of our lives remains the same. And our task is to spread the love of God throughout the world. God's light needs to be shone in remote corners of the globe, but it is also desperately needed in our own backyards. Our own cities, towns, schools, and neighborhoods are full of hurting people who need Jesus.

Think of a few ways you can spread Jesus's love. They can be small or large, something to do today or something to work toward in the future. Keep focused on these tasks, no matter how much uncertainty wants to crowd out your motivation.

DAY 317

"The plans of the diligent lead to profit as surely as haste leads to poverty."

—PROVERBS 21:5

There are a lot of cool, exciting things vying for our attention every day. We live in an age of flashing lights—both literally and figuratively speaking. It would be easy to allow the fun stuff, all those new and shiny diversions, to swallow up our days. You could live an entire lifetime hopping from one distraction to the next.

But God wants us to plan wisely and well. He wants us to consider the future and live not just for today but with a long game in mind. He wants us to be profitable in building his church—growing in him and helping others to grow. He wants us to be known as good employees, diligent students, and people who make wise decisions in our lives. Earning a reputation like that requires thinking beyond just the "right now."

What sort of plans do you have for the next year or two? What about the next five or ten? Pray about some areas where you want to further develop your long game.

DAY 318

"For if you remain silent at this time, relief and deliverance for the Jews will arise from another place, but you and your father's family will perish. And who knows but that you have come to your royal position for such a time as this?"

—ESTHER 4:14

Have you ever wondered what God's will is for your life? If so, you're not alone. Esther faced that question in a very big way. As a young woman, she was in the very peculiar position of being queen to the king that held her people (the Jews) in captivity. Nefarious plots to destroy the Jews were under way, and it was up to Esther to speak to the king about it. One small snag. Speaking to the king without being summoned first could get Esther killed. But *not* speaking to the king would certainly get her people killed. Yikes.

But as Esther's uncle points out here, God had placed her in this unusual and scary position to serve as deliverer of her people—who also happened to be God's people. We don't always have roles quite this grand. Most of us don't have the fate of a nation resting on our shoulders. But we do serve the same God Esther did. And, like Esther, God positions us to serve him in unique ways. Seize the opportunities God puts before you. Search for open doors, and see what the Lord has planned for you on the other side.

DAY 319

"'For I know the plans I have for you,' declares the LORD, *'plans to prosper you and not to harm you, plans to give you hope and a future.'"*

—JEREMIAH 29:11

Okay, so maybe we diligently plan for the future. Maybe we look for all the open doors God has put before us and, with his blessing, we run through those doors to discover what's on the other side. Maybe we spend long periods of time in prayer, hoping to discern God's will for our futures. If we do all those things, God will never shut doors for us, right? Er . . . not exactly.

The truth is, God often shuts doors. Sometimes it's easy to understand why he shuts a door. The path is no longer a healthy or productive one so he steers us in a different direction. Other times, it's a little harder to understand. Perhaps the process of thinking we were going to walk through that door was important for some reason. Perhaps we grew in some way because of that experience.

But whatever the *why,* we can always be sure that God has a plan for our lives. When he shuts our doors, we don't need to be dismayed. He will open another door—or maybe a window—and show us the next step in his beautiful plan.

"But it is the spirit in a person, the breath of the Almighty, that gives them understanding."

—JOB 32:8

All throughout history, women have given a lot of time and attention to their outer appearances. Our modern era is certainly no exception. If anything, we're even more focused on such things. It's easy to buy into the idea that our outward appearance is extremely important.

And our bodies truly are good creations—wonderful gifts from God that can be used to glorify him. But what do you think matters more to God, a beautiful face or a beautiful heart? God cares about our inward appearance more than our outer shells.

Think about how much time and energy you usually devote to outward appearances. How much time is spent on hair, makeup, clothes, and keeping in shape? None of these things is bad. But what does it reveal when we compare it to how much time we devote to our inner appearances? Think of ten new ways you can sharpen your mind, deepen your faith, enrich your prayer life, or grow in another inward area. You're God's daughter—and that means you're beautiful inside and out.

DAY 321

"And you will receive a rich welcome into the eternal kingdom of our Lord and Savior Jesus Christ."

—2 PETER 1:11

Have you ever heard the expression "You can't take it with you"? It means that when you die, you can't take any of your material possessions with you, so you shouldn't put too much focus on them in this life. In the long run, they don't really matter. It's a wise saying!

Sometimes we get so caught up in the material possessions of this world, they can become our primary focus. We want a bigger house, a nicer car, sparklier jewelry. While these possessions are nice to have, how much more important are the things that endure into eternity? *People* endure. Souls endure. And after the resurrection, our bodies will endure for eternity. These are the things we *can* take with us.

Thank God today for the gift of the eternity of your soul. Rescuing that eternal piece of you was the first purpose of the cross, and it's amazing to realize just how much God must love us.

DAY 322

"Sell your possessions and give to the poor. Provide purses for yourselves that will not wear out, a treasure in heaven that will never fail, where no thief comes near and no moth destroys."

—LUKE 12:33

While we know that God wants us to be mindful of our lives here on earth and our future plans, it's also clear that those who follow Jesus should live life with the soul in mind. But what does that mean?

For us, that means not getting caught up in the material world. God's earth is a wonderful thing, and we're blessed to live in an age where we enjoy unprecedented levels of fun and excitement. Our lives are, for the most part, easier than the billions of people who lived before us. But sometimes these fun, exciting things become distractions and we forget to live with the soul in mind. We forget that salvation is the most important gift we can share with others. We forget that our souls and the souls of others should be top priority in our lives.

Think of a few ways you can reprioritize your life so that you're living with the soul at the top of your priority list.

DAY 323

"See, I will create new heavens and a new earth. The former things will not be remembered, nor will they come to mind."

—ISAIAH 65:17

We are so used to our physical bodies. They're real—they're here and now and we can see and touch them. We're also used to the cycle of life. Birth and death seem to be the natural ways of the world. And they are—*now.*

But God's creation was originally eternal. The earth was created to last forever. Plants, animals, and human beings were created as part of God's eternal kingdom. That original design was corrupted by sin, and creation had to get used to a new definition of natural—one that included death of all living things.

So the new heaven and new earth God has promised to create—the one that will be sin-free and last for eternity—isn't some weird afterthought, added like an odd bit of punctuation on the end of God's ideas. It's the original idea being restored to its full glory. How amazing is it that we will someday get to experience the excellent plan God had in mind from the beginning?

DAY 324

"For where two or three gather in my name, there am I with them."

—MATTHEW 18:20

Eternity is such a wonderful promise. All of forever without sickness, death, or pain. And, even better, sin won't be messing with the picture anymore. That means everything we do, everything we say, will be a perfect act of worship toward God. No distractions, nothing pulling us toward unwise decisions or potential pitfalls. Hallelujah!

But we don't have to wait for eternity. We can reflect this deep, heartfelt praise of God here and now. In fact, that's what churches are for. Churches are built around the idea of worshiping God. When we sharpen our minds by listening to sermons, lift our voices in song, serve one another and our communities, we reflect what we have to look forward to in eternity.

We may not be able to praise God perfectly here and now, but we can certainly bring glory to him and growth to our lives by loving God's church as much as he does.

DAY 325

"There is a time for everything, and a season for every activity under the heavens."

—ECCLESIASTES 3:1

"This too shall pass." Lots of people think that phrase comes from the Bible, but it doesn't. Not in those words, anyway. But the Bible does talk about seasons, and seasons come and go in our lives. So it's not too far off to say that the Bible reflects the idea that "this too shall pass."

When we're dealing with difficult circumstances, those words can serve as a comfort. No difficulty lasts forever. We go through times of hardship, and we go through times of blessing. We go through times that are wildly exciting and times that are inescapably dull. We go through times when life feels full and times when it feels empty.

Enjoy the great seasons of your life. Persevere through the difficult ones. No season lasts forever. This too shall pass.

DAY 326

"He went away a second time and prayed, 'My Father, if it is not possible for this cup to be taken away unless I drink it, may your will be done.'"

—MATTHEW 26:42

Do you love to pray? Is it something that comes super easily to you? Or do you have to remind yourself to spend some time each day talking to God?

Whether you're a natural at praying or you have to work a little harder at it, everyone can learn to pray better by keeping an eternal perspective. When we keep eternity in view—when we understand that earthly seasons are short-lived and we are created for something much more enduring—it is easier to pray as Jesus did. Not my will, God, but *yours* be done.

Praying for God's will in our lives can be very scary. Letting go of control, letting go of our desires and giving them over to God, might even feel like a freefall. But God's got us. He has control, and that's infinitely more important than gripping our hopes in our tiny little fists, willing them to happen. God has the big-picture plan, so we can find freedom in releasing our lives to him.

DAY 327

"And the Levites . . . said: 'Stand up and praise the LORD your God, who is from everlasting to everlasting. Blessed be your glorious name, and may it be exalted above all blessing and praise.'"

—NEHEMIAH 9:5

Perhaps God's will for our lives is that we are in a position of influence, whether that be in school, work, our own families, or in our future careers. Having influence is a pretty awesome thing—and something to be taken seriously. It's quite a huge responsibility to make sure you're taking care of the people looking to you for leadership.

It's important we don't let our positions of influence cause us to lose perspective. No matter how large our worldly influence—even if we're running an entire nation—it pales in comparison to God's eternal, everlasting power. It's very tempting for those in leadership to forget this. Power and influence can tempt us to believe we're indestructible.

If you find yourself as an influencer, guard your heart against this temptation. And thank God for the blessing of good leaders in your life, whether they're teachers, pastors, government officials, or your parents. It's not an easy job to be in charge, and our leaders could always use your prayers!

"So don't be afraid; you are worth more than many sparrows."

—MATTHEW 10:31

God sees you as an everlasting creation. You haven't always been in existence, but from the moment you were brought to life, you had an everlasting soul. That soul matters to God. Jesus moved heaven and earth to keep that soul from everlasting destruction. God calls you to him so that your soul will find everlasting blessing instead.

And that everlasting blessing—that everlasting life—is not something we have to wait for. It doesn't just start when we die or when Jesus returns. It starts the moment we accept Jesus as savior. We grow in the image of Jesus, becoming more and more like him, here on earth. We have peace and faith and trust in God here on earth. We can *know* God here and now. These are all aspects of everlasting life we can participate in during our lifetimes.

Grab hold of more life today. God wants you to have it—the deepest relationship with him possible.

DAY 329

"Don't let anyone look down on you because you are young, but set an example for the believers in speech, in conduct, in love, in faith and in purity."

—1 TIMOTHY 4:12

Age seems to make a big difference in our linear, time-bound world. There are appropriate ages for lots of different life milestones—being a student, getting married, becoming a parent, traveling the world. The list goes on.

But age doesn't matter so much to God. He sees you now as a young woman but he also sees you in ten, twenty, or sixty years. Even if we live to be a hundred years old, what's a hundred years to God? Just a blink.

This is good news for us. It means you don't have to wait for some marker of age to be passed. You can begin setting an example in your life, serving and ministering to others, today. Right now. It doesn't matter if you're twenty or twelve. You're not disqualified. So what are you waiting for?

DAY 330

"Blessed is the one who perseveres under trial because, having stood the test, that person will receive the crown of life that the Lord has promised to those who love him."

—JAMES 1:12

Imagine you see some warm chocolate chip cookies sitting on the kitchen counter. They smell amazing. They're fresh out of the oven. Just the way you like them. But—ack!—you remember Mom made those cookies for a church event. You're not supposed to have any. And she'll be really upset if you swipe one. She made *just* enough and she needs all of them. You can either eat a cookie and hope you get away with it (danger!), or you can think about the consequences you will face for getting caught and skip the cookie.

If you skip the cookie, you're thinking long term. You're not just focusing on the amazing smell or tempting gooey chips. You're thinking about consequences and what's right and wrong. It's the same with sin in our lives. Sin is never a delicious cookie, but it sure looks like it when we're tempted. When you feel tempted to do something you know is wrong, think long term to help you flee that temptation.

"The God who made the world and everything in it is the Lord of heaven and earth and does not live in temples built by human hands. And he is not served by human hands, as if he needed anything. Rather, he himself gives everyone life and breath and everything else."

—ACTS 17:24–25

A lot of modern cultures value independence. We hold freedom and individuality in high regard, and maybe that's because independence is one of the attributes of our Creator. God's independence means he doesn't need anything or anyone. He is fully free of need.

Wait. Does that mean God has, literally, no use for us? Should we be offended? It doesn't sound nice at first, but it's actually pretty cool. God doesn't *need* us, but he still *wants* us. God's independence should humble us, yes, but it can also remind us just how loved we are. That's an amazing truth!

DAY 332

"For every animal of the forest is mine, and the cattle on a thousand hills. I know every bird in the mountains, and the insects in the fields are mine. If I were hungry I would not tell you, for the world is mine, and all that is in it."

—PSALM 50:10–12

The whole world belongs to God. Every leaf on every tree is his. Every bit of fur on all the snuggly animals (and the not-so-snuggly ones too) belongs to him. And if God keeps track of every leaf, all the fur, each tree, and every animal, we can be sure he's also keeping track of all people. That, of course, includes you.

Can you imagine being responsible for all that detail—all that life, all those souls? It's truly a responsibility only God could fulfill. God doesn't share the immensity of his burden with us. He doesn't put his worries on our shoulders. Instead, he carries *our* burdens and soothes *our* worries for us. That's some serious love.

God is free to do whatever he wishes. If he wanted, he could have spun the world into motion and then walked away, leaving us to fend for ourselves. But he *chose* not to. He chose to stay near to his beloved creation—to love us, support us, and be responsible for us.

"And now, Father, glorify me in your presence with the glory I had with you before the world began."

—JOHN 17:5

The trinity of Father, Son, and Holy Spirit is one of the more abstract spiritual truths to try to understand. God is one essence but three persons. He's never been lonely. But he created human beings, and gave us family and friends to spend our time with here on earth.

Think about the most important, treasured relationships in your life. Your parents, your friends, your siblings—these relationships may not be perfect, but the love you share with these special people is a direct reflection of God's gift to us. He doesn't want us to be lonely. Relationships are one of God's most joyous blessings. Enjoy them!

DAY 334

"God said to Moses, 'I AM WHO I AM. This is what you are to say to the Israelites: "I AM has sent me to you."'"

—EXODUS 3:14

We're dependent on so many things throughout our lives. In fact, humans enter the world as pretty helpless. Unlike some animals, we must have someone care for us—feed us, clothe us, protect us—or we won't survive infancy. That's just a fact of being human. Even after we grow up and can care for ourselves, the conditions necessary to support life are pretty specific. We need just the right atmosphere, water, and a fair amount of food. And those are just the basics!

God is not like us. He does not depend on others to care for him. He doesn't need oxygen to breathe, food to eat, or water to drink. There is literally nothing else on earth or in heaven like God. Before you pray today, pause to think about that for a minute. We worship a Creator who far surpasses our limited understanding. He is unique in his independence and boundless in his love.

DAY 335

"Everyone who is called by my name, whom I created for my glory, whom I formed and made."

—ISAIAH 43:7

Thinking about God's greatness can inspire truly deep, heartfelt worship and gratitude. Or . . . it can inspire feelings of smallness. Insignificance. Worthlessness. After all, if God is so big, so great, and needs nothing from me, how much can we possibly matter?

Oh, but God doesn't see it that way. The very simple truth is that God decided we matter, therefore we do. No further proof required. He says we're called. He says he made us. And he says we were created *for his glory*. Are we small? Yes. Are we weak? Often. But do we still matter? Absolutely! We bring glory to the one true God. Our lives show others how God can transform people, shape people, build people into living signposts that point to Jesus. That certainly doesn't sound insignificant!

So remember why you were created and why you were called—to bring glory to God with your thoughts, words, and actions.

DAY 336

"I am the vine; you are the branches. If you remain in me and I in you, you will bear much fruit; apart from me you can do nothing."

—JOHN 15:5

Have you ever been in a situation where you've worked hard, perhaps as part of a team, but someone else took all the credit? Ouch. That stings. It can be hard not to be recognized for our accomplishments. Especially when someone else is taking the credit.

In spite of the sting, we can learn an important lesson from these experiences. When we become too focused on taking credit, we're missing the point of the gifts God has given to us. God wants us to be part of the big picture—humble contributors who glorify *him*, rather than draw attention to ourselves.

God wants us to use our strength, wisdom, creativity, and holiness in our lives. Those attributes are wonderful, and God wants us to display them. But we must recognize that he is the source of any talent or virtue we possess. It helps keep us from getting addicted to the attention and affirmation our accomplishments can bring us.

DAY 337

"Let us not become weary in doing good, for at the proper time we will reap a harvest if we do not give up."

—GALATIANS 6:9

Have you ever walked along the beach? Your feet leave behind an impression in the wet sand as you walk along. The landscape is changed because you were there. You've left a physical impact.

Each of us leaves a spiritual impact on the world around us too. And unlike a wet footprint on the beach, our impact can be lasting. Helping others, giving to those in need, showing honesty and integrity, and exercising self-control are all good deeds that have a positive impact on the world around us—whether you're in school, at home, or just hanging out with friends. Your surrounding landscape is changed by these good "footprints." People are affected.

And impacting your world for good brings glory to God. Each of those footprints left by a selfless deed has God's name on it. Think about how you can create godly footprints in your world today.

DAY 338

"As a young man marries a young woman, so will your Builder marry you; as a bridegroom rejoices over his bride, so will your God rejoice over you."

—ISAIAH 62:5

What are some things in your life that cause you to rejoice? Maybe you find joy in your relationships with family and friends. Your hobbies, favorite foods, and pets probably bring you happiness too. These blessings are meant to enrich our lives!

Did you know that *you* bring joy to God? That's right. God rejoices over you. It's one of his great, wonderful mysteries. He doesn't need us, but he chooses us, and we have the ability to bring him joy. And when we talk about God's joy, we're not talking about the fleeting happiness that comes from winning a big game, acing a test, or eating an excellent chocolate-chip cookie, though all those things are pretty awesome. Especially the cookie. Because . . . cookies.

No, we're talking about something bigger than happiness. True, deep joy. We bring God joy with every step of growth we take. Every bit of spiritual maturity we gain causes him to rejoice.

"The Lord *your God is with you, the Mighty Warrior who saves. He will take great delight in you; in his love he will no longer rebuke you, but will rejoice over you with singing."*

—ZEPHANIAH 3:17

We know that God wants us to show love to others. When Jesus summed up the whole of the law, he said the main themes were to love God and love others. When we love others, God rejoices over us.

So what are some practical ways to love people? The possibilities are endless, but here are a few ideas. You can babysit so a busy mom can go grocery shopping by herself. You can offer a listening ear to your friend who is struggling through a tough time. You can partner with your church or a local ministry to get nonperishable foods or other essentials to the homeless in your area. You can make (or purchase) a meal for the family at church with a new baby. You can volunteer to clean the facilities at church one Saturday a month.

Can you think of other ways to tangibly show love to those around you? God rejoices over these gestures, no matter how simple.

DAY 340

"In the same way, let your light shine before others, that they may see your good deeds and glorify your Father in heaven."

—MATTHEW 5:16

Accomplishing our goals can be a thrilling experience. When we set our minds to something—whether it's a top grade in a tough class, the lead in the school play, or having a great season in our favorite sport—achieving those targets feels wonderful. And it should! We work hard to accomplish these things.

It's okay to celebrate our accomplishments. But it's even better when God is part of that celebration. When we acknowledge God as the source of our talents and skills, and that we're able to achieve our goals because of his blessings on our lives, we bring him joy. Not only do we bring God joy, we draw other people's attention to him. We glorify him.

So keep aiming high. Keep scaling those mountains. Just remember to thank the one who gives you the strength to climb!

DAY 341

"But when the kindness and love of God our Savior appeared, he saved us, not because of righteous things we had done, but because of his mercy. He saved us through the washing of rebirth and renewal by the Holy Spirit."

—TITUS 3:4–5

The Gospel is as simple as these two sentences from Titus. Simple, yet we could spend our whole lives studying it and its impact on our lives and still not fully grasp it all. God's truths are like that.

When we share this simple yet complex good news with others, we bring God joy. This is one of the main ways the kingdom of God grows. We tell others about Jesus's sacrifice on the cross, they believe, and new disciples are made—new brothers and sisters are brought into the kingdom. There is, perhaps, nothing that brings God more joy. Because new brothers and sisters for us mean new sons and daughters for God.

There are lots of ways to tell people about Jesus. Sometimes it's those few sentences that lay out God's plan for salvation. Sometimes we "tell" people through our actions—living out our faith in ways others can see and then they can't help but wonder about our peace, joy, and love. However God leads you to share, know that when you expand the kingdom, you bring him joy.

DAY 342

"Do nothing out of selfish ambition or vain conceit. Rather, in humility value others above yourselves."

—PHILIPPIANS 2:3

If you've spent much time around young children, you know what fun they can be. New experiences are delightful when you see them through the eyes of little kids. Things that have become mundane or even tiresome to us can be given new life when we rediscover them with a young child. If you don't believe me, find a toddler who is fascinated with a vacuum cleaner.

But if you spend time around little kids, you also know something else about human nature: we don't need to be taught to be selfish. Little ones are precious, but they're also naturally inclined to think of their own needs first. Honestly? Most of us continue to struggle with selfishness for the rest of our lives, at least to some degree.

And that's why sacrificial love is such an amazing thing—and one of the best, hardest callings God gives to his children. We're told to value other people above ourselves. It's downright unnatural! But it's glorious in action. Putting others first reflects Jesus's sacrifice on the cross where he put *us* first. That kind of reflection brings God great joy.

DAY 343

"And he has filled him with the Spirit of God, with wisdom, with understanding, with knowledge and with all kinds of skills— to make artistic designs for work in gold, silver and bronze."

—EXODUS 35:31–32

God loves creativity. He is the ultimate Creator. And all we have to do is look around at this big, beautiful world to see his handiwork. He made oceans, plants, animals, stars—and even *us*.

It makes sense that God enjoys our creativity. Our desire to make things is one aspect of his thumbprint on us. Creativity can take many forms. Some of us like to paint or draw. Others like to tell stories or write plays. Some like to dream up new recipes. Maybe there are some crafters among us who crochet, knit, or sew. Creativity can come in the form of building, woodworking, and technological innovation too. Architecture, interior design, theater, dance, music—it all takes creativity!

What's your favorite way to show that God-spark inside you? Think of how you can grow your skills in that area.

DAY 344

"A cheerful heart is good medicine, but a crushed spirit dries up the bones."

—PROVERBS 17:22

Do you ever feel like bringing God joy must be hard work? Combatting our own selfishness, working to put others first, leaving a positive impact on the world—these things are excellent pursuits and very worth the effort. But they're just that—effort. Work.

Not everything that brings God joy is hard work for us, though. God is joyful when we celebrate. God is pleased when we experience life. God smiles on us when we find laughter. It's true that our lives won't always be sunshine and roses and rainbows and kittens. But it's also true that our lives *do* include sunshine and roses and rainbows and kittens at times. And it's a wonderful thing to celebrate the good, positive things God brings into our lives.

The life of a Jesus-follower can be tough. Not everyone understands faith. So celebrating the positive not only brings joy to God, it can help carry us through our toughest times. Don't be afraid to enjoy life and find your laughter.

DAY 345

"As soon as Jesus was baptized, he went up out of the water. At that moment heaven was opened, and he saw the Spirit of God descending like a dove and alighting on him. And a voice from heaven said, 'This is my Son, whom I love; with him I am well pleased.'"

—MATTHEW 3:16–17

Maybe it's so obvious, it goes without saying. But sometimes those obvious truths are the easiest to miss, so they're worth pointing out. God was extremely pleased with his son, Jesus.

Too obvious? Maybe. Of course God was pleased with Jesus. Of course his perfectly obedient son brought him joy. So maybe it also goes without saying that when we act like Jesus, God finds joy in us.

Obvious or not, it's the truth. So when we read about Jesus's life in the Bible, we should always be thinking about ways to become more like him. Jesus loved others. He put God first. He submitted to God's plan for his life, even when it was difficult—*especially* when it was difficult. Jesus always spoke truth. What other characteristics of Jesus would you like to emulate? How can you better reflect Jesus to bring God joy?

DAY 346

"Where can I go from your Spirit? Where can I flee from your presence? If I go up to the heavens, you are there; if I make my bed in the depths, you are there."

—PSALM 139:7–8

Have you ever noticed that a lot of times we use the word "literally" when we actually mean the opposite? A friend says something hilarious, and we may respond, "I literally just died laughing." But of course that means you *figuratively* died laughing. Which is good news, because that'd be a bizarre way to go, and we don't want to limit ourselves to unfunny friends. You know, just in case.

It's not misusing the word to say that God is literally everywhere. He is, in the truest sense of the word, *everywhere*. In all places at all times. It even has a fancy Latin word—*omnipresent*. That's why David wrote in his psalm that there was nowhere he could go to run away from God. It's impossible to flee from God's presence. And that's not a bad thing. When we recognize that our God is good, just, holy, and loving, we understand that constantly being in his presence is an excellent blessing.

DAY 347

"For in him all things were created: things in heaven and on earth, visible and invisible, whether thrones or powers or rulers or authorities; all things have been created through him and for him."

—COLOSSIANS 1:16

Certain aspects of God's character are more confusing than others. God's holiness and his wisdom are pretty easy to understand, for example. There are many straightforward examples of God's holiness and wisdom in Scripture, and we can see his words firsthand in the Bible.

But other traits are harder for us to grasp. Omnipresence is one of those. It's easy to think of God as filling up the biggest space there is, but he isn't actually contained in any space at all. Space is something God created, so there's no space large enough or old enough to contain him. And yet . . . he is everywhere. It's enough to twist our minds up in knots if we think about it too long.

A simple way to think about God's omnipresence is that he is *present* in but *separate* from his creation—sort of like water in a sponge. He is in us—in all of creation—without being limited to one place, one person, or one time.

DAY 348

"'Am I only a God nearby,' declares the LORD, 'and not a God far away? Who can hide in secret places so that I cannot see them?' declares the LORD. 'Do not I fill heaven and earth?' declares the LORD."

—JEREMIAH 23:23–24

There are a lot of limits placed on our behavior from the outside. Rules at school are designed to keep order for students and teachers. Rules at home are in place to help your parents raise you with the values they want and teach you responsibility. The laws of the land keep everyone in order and punish those who don't stick with the program. Pretty much anywhere you find people, you'll find rules to help control people's actions.

But we still have secret moments. Times when we're alone. Times when no one is looking. Times when we can break a rule—and maybe even get away with it, if we're sneaky enough.

Except for one pesky fact: there's no hiding from God. He sees every action—every single thing we do, no matter where we are or who's around. And we know our actions matter to God. So in those secret moments when we're tempted to act in ways we shouldn't, remember that God is there with you.

DAY 349

"But I tell you that everyone will have to give account on the day of judgment for every empty word they have spoken. For by your words you will be acquitted, and by your words you will be condemned."

—MATTHEW 12:36–37

Have you ever posted something on social media, then immediately regretted it? Have you ever been extremely thankful for the "delete" and "edit" buttons? Sometimes the Internet lets us take back our words. Other times, they're out there forever, so it's really important to be cautious and wise about what we say on the Internet.

Words that we actually say, however, don't come with a delete option. Once they've been said and heard, we can say we didn't mean it, try to explain our point of view further, or say we've changed our minds, but we can't undo the words that were spoken. In the process, we can damage relationships or face other consequences.

How much more carefully do you think you would guard your words if you thought about God being right there beside you? Because he is. Our words matter to him. Let your knowledge of God's omnipresence help you guard your words carefully.

DAY 350

"Finally, brothers and sisters, whatever is true, whatever is noble, whatever is right, whatever is pure, whatever is lovely, whatever is admirable—if anything is excellent or praiseworthy—think about such things."

—PHILIPPIANS 4:8

It's possible to control our behavior most of the time. Maybe we've even become pretty good at guarding the words that come out of our mouths. So that means we're in the clear, right? Not exactly. We can usually hide our thoughts from others, but not God. He's not just everywhere around us—he's actually inside us, able to know our thoughts and feelings.

Did that just make you freak out a little? If it did, you're not alone. The idea of anyone, let alone our holy God, being able to know *everything* that ever passes through our brains is a little overwhelming. We have a hard enough job just controlling our actions and our words. Thoughts seem to fire through our minds unbidden sometimes, so how can we possibly control those?

But God's Word tells us to think about things that are true, noble, right, pure, lovely, admirable, excellent, and praiseworthy. We *can* grow to have some measure of control over our thoughts by focusing on these good, godly things.

DAY 351

"Don't you see that whatever enters the mouth goes into the stomach and then out of the body? But the things that come out of a person's mouth come from the heart, and these defile them. For out of the heart come evil thoughts."

—MATTHEW 15:17–19A

Jesus brought up matters of the heart often during his earthly ministry. He was the originator of "practice what you preach," and for people to first practice what they preached, their hearts needed to be in the right place. Jesus constantly called out religious hypocrisy—those leaders who talked a lot about holiness and following God but whose hearts were very, very far away from God. Jesus knew the heart was way more important than how a person looked on the outside.

And all of those principles apply to us today too. Our hearts not only matter to God, but they probably matter *most*. Our heart speaks to our intent—our motives. Our heart speaks to all the most secret things we hide from everyone. And *that* piece of us is what concerned Jesus the most.

Eep. The good news is that we can work on our hearts by praying often and walking the way Jesus did—by putting others before ourselves. Over time, as we grow in holiness, the darkness in our hearts lessens. We reflect God better, inch by inch.

DAY 352

"You make known to me the path of life; you will fill me with joy in your presence, with eternal pleasures at your right hand."

—PSALM 16:11

Have you ever had a time in your life where you just *knew* God was with you? Maybe you felt his strength during a difficult move, your parents' divorce, or the death of a loved one. Maybe you felt his tender patience when you were wrestling with your faith or asking deep, spiritual questions. Or maybe God answered a prayer you thought was, for sure, a longshot. Those moments can reinforce what we always know to be true—that God is *here* with us.

But even when we don't feel it as strongly, God is still there. Sometimes his purposes don't involve a particular blessing or a special intervention, but he is always there, beside us and in us. Try keeping a journal of all the times you've strongly felt God's presence in your life. You might be surprised how often it is!

DAY 353

"He is before all things, and in him all things hold together."

—COLOSSIANS 1:17

Walking with Jesus is full of big events—accepting Jesus, getting baptized, trusting God, and stepping out in faith for the first time. These events are wonderful milestones to be celebrated, but walking with Jesus is also about the *process.* Studying the Bible is a process. Learning how to pray is a process. Growing in maturity is a process. The day in, day out process of following Jesus is as important as the big milestones.

God's presence is like that too. We read many stories in the Bible where God's presence is there to bless someone, and we read some stories where his presence is there to punish someone who has rejected him. Those are big events. But what about all the other days—literally, millions of them—where God's presence didn't show up in a loud way? Was he still there?

Absolutely. God is always there, even when he's not doing something loud. He is constantly sustaining creation, including us. He holds the fabric of the universe together, giving us air to breathe, life to live. And he's always listening. Remember God's presence in the quiet moments too.

DAY 354

"When you pass through the waters, I will be with you; and when you pass through the rivers, they will not sweep over you. When you walk through the fire, you will not be burned; the flames will not set you ablaze."

—ISAIAH 43:2

Have you ever felt like God is very far away? We may know with our minds that God is always with us, but sometimes when we go through dark times, it feels like God couldn't be further away. We may even feel like he's left us for good.

Have you ever been there? Maybe you lost a good friend at some point. Or maybe your family has been through really difficult times. Maybe you've faced intense peer pressure at school or been bullied in person or online. Those could all be described as "passing through rivers" or "walking through fire."

But we don't need to feel abandoned. God has promised he will *always* be with us. Sometimes he rescues us from the fire in amazing ways. But other times, he walks through the fire beside us, allowing us to experience it but protecting us from burns. You are *not* alone, and you never will be.

DAY 355

"And surely I am with you always, to the very end of the age."

—MATTHEW 28:20B

Sometimes we feel like God is far away because we're going through really hard times that are out of our control. Other times, God feels far away because we've pulled away from him. And still other times, we've not only pulled away from him but we've shoved him and run screaming in the other direction.

Can you relate? Often when we want to run screaming from God, it's because we know we're about to do something that would displease him. Ouch. That's a tough truth. And of course there are other reasons why we may feel far from God. But it's always worth taking a hard look at your life and asking if sin is the reason you're feeling far from God's presence.

The good news is that God won't abandon us to our wrong choices or bad habits. All we have to do is turn away from our sins, and God welcomes us back with open arms.

DAY 356

"About three in the afternoon Jesus cried out in a loud voice, 'Eli, Eli, lema sabachthani?' (which means 'My God, my God, why have you forsaken me?')."

—MATTHEW 27:46

Do you ever read about heroes in the Bible and feel a little inadequate? If so, you're not alone. Sometimes it's easy to get the impression that the people of great faith who came before us were perfectly obedient and far more righteous than we'll ever be. Then, of course, there's Jesus, who actually was perfect and whose example we're told to follow. It feels beyond impossible!

But when it comes to feeling alone—like God has abandoned us—we never need to feel like our faith heroes couldn't relate. Scripture is full of examples of people of great faith who wondered why God had left them. Job and David asked this question, but our most outstanding example is Jesus, himself.

What! It's true. As Jesus hung on the cross, he called out the words of one of David's psalms and asked, "God, why have you left me?" That's right. God's own son. Luckily, the story and the psalm don't end there. The psalm goes on to talk about the Lord delivering David, and Jesus ultimately defeated death. When you feel most alone, remember that God isn't finished telling your story.

DAY 357

"He went out to meet Asa and said to him, 'Listen to me, Asa and all Judah and Benjamin. The Lord *is with you when you are with him. If you seek him, he will be found by you, but if you forsake him, he will forsake you.'"*

—2 CHRONICLES 15:2

Everyone faces battles in life. Some of them are on a grand scale—battles against oppression or discrimination or pressure from society. Some of them are more individual—battles against a particular sin we struggle with, a battle against a health condition or another disadvantage. And some of us will face actual physical battles.

And each of those battles can feel like a dragon. Do you ever feel like a lone knight marching toward that massive beast with little hope to slay it? Or maybe you feel more like a damsel locked in a tower without a sword or shield to help you. That can be even scarier!

Whenever you march out to face your battles, remember that God is with you. Not only will he not leave you, but he's helping you face that dragon. God is with us through our battles, through our defeats, and through our victories.

DAY 358

"By day the Lord *went ahead of them in a pillar of cloud to guide them on their way and by night in a pillar of fire to give them light, so that they could travel by day or night."*

—EXODUS 13:21

Maybe it seems crazy for us to imagine the Israelites experienced God's presence in such a physical way. A pillar of fire led them at night and a pillar of cloud led them by day as they traveled through the wilderness. But in their culture and era, it wasn't such a foreign idea to have a physical representation of an invisible God. That's exactly what their neighbors' idols were.

In our day and age, we might not be as tempted by physical representations of gods as the Israelites were. But we can wander into the opposite error. Because God is invisible and not contained in a body or a building, we might think that our buildings and spaces don't matter to him. But just like with Solomon's temple or Moses's tabernacle, God is delighted by the physical spaces we use to worship him. Those spaces may not contain him, but they are dedicated to him. Whether it's a beautiful cathedral, a modest building, or even a rented public space or a brand-new church that meets in a home, God is honored by our gathering in a particular place in his name.

DAY 359

"Pray continually."

—1 THESSALONIANS 5:17

Have you ever felt intimidated by prayer? A lot of people are nervous about praying in front of others (*what if I say something wrong?!*), but even the idea of approaching God privately can be a little overwhelming. This is God we're talking about, after all. Besides . . . how do we talk to someone we can't see? Is he even listening?

And yet, the Bible tells us to pray continuously. The thing is, God *is* really there. Prayer isn't a formality or a ceremony where God is waiting for you to say the right—or wrong—thing. It's a conversation. God knows all our thoughts, even before we've processed them, so we don't have to pray in order for him to know what we need. But he tells us to anyway. That's because this conversation between us and him is for our benefit. Prayer helps us practice humility, process our thoughts and emotions, and to acknowledge that God is with us—right there, listening, responding.

Pray continually, the Bible tells us. It's not just a formality; it's a necessity!

DAY 360

"And without faith it is impossible to please God, because anyone who comes to him must believe that he exists and that he rewards those who earnestly seek him."

—HEBREWS 11:6

Have you ever had a hiccup in your prayer life? Maybe you used to be in a solid routine of communicating with God, but life got in the way and suddenly you find yourself out of the habit. Maybe *way* out of the habit, to the point that you don't remember how you ever had time to pray in the first place. You're certainly not the only one to find herself in that position!

Don't worry. There are ways to reconnect and jump-start that conversation with God again. It can help to remember God's promises to us. He promises to save us. He promises never to leave us. He promises to help us and to love us. Reminding ourselves of the deep, true love behind these promises can draw us back into an awareness of his presence.

No matter how busy you are this week, schedule some time to sit down with God. Don't give up on seeking him or building your relationship with him through prayer.

DAY 361

"Peter replied, 'Repent and be baptized, every one of you, in the name of Jesus Christ for the forgiveness of your sins. And you will receive the gift of the Holy Spirit.'"

—ACTS 2:38

If God is everywhere, does that mean he is "with" those who don't believe in him? Do believers have God's presence in a different sense than those who don't believe in Jesus?

God truly is with everyone in the broadest sense. He sustains all of creation, and that includes people who don't acknowledge him. But believers have a very special gift of God's presence. Believers have God's own Spirit in them. God is with everyone, but he's with us in a very special way. The Holy Spirit helps guide us. He makes us aware of God's leading, helps us understand the Bible, and infuses God's law into our consciences.

The Holy Spirit is one of the greatest gifts God gives to followers of Jesus. Take an extra moment today to thank God for that unique blessing of God's presence in your heart.

DAY 362

"'Pardon me, my lord,' Gideon replied, 'but how can I save Israel? My clan is the weakest in Manasseh, and I am the least in my family.' The LORD answered, 'I will be with you.'"

—JUDGES 6:15–16A

Have you ever had a big challenge staring you in the face—an important test, a big game, a huge project, or perhaps something that could have an impact on your future, like a college entrance exam? Those challenges can be exciting—and very scary. When it feels like we have a lot riding on our performance, it's easy to feel overwhelmed and alone.

Gideon could relate. He had the challenge of saving his entire nation staring him in the face. And like us, he wondered, "How in the world will I be able to do this?" Maybe he even felt alone.

But we're not alone. Ever. Our God is always with us, just as he promised to be with Gideon. God said to Gideon, "Go. I'm sending you, aren't I? I will be with you." And he whispers to us, "I'm with you, aren't I? Go for it. Don't be afraid!"

DAY 363

"The grace of the Lord Jesus Christ be with your spirit."

—PHILEMON 25

Have you ever had a friend you were really close with—the kind of friend who you've spent countless hours with? Her house is your second home, and vice versa. You can practically finish each other sentences, and you basically know what she's thinking all the time. A true BFF.

Have you noticed that if you spend a ton of time with someone, you tend to pick up on their quirks, habits, or mannerisms? Or maybe they pick up yours. That's because spending many hours in someone's presence tends to change you. When we're talking human to human, it changes both of you, which is why it's a good idea to surround yourself with good friends who share your values.

When we make a point to be aware of God's presence in our lives—and we spend lots of time soaking in that awareness of God's presence—we can't help but be changed by him. And when we're being changed by God, you know we're being changed for the better. God's presence grows us, strengthens us, matures us.

DAY 364

"And I heard a loud voice from the throne saying, 'Look! God's dwelling place is now among the people, and he will dwell with them. They will be his people, and God himself will be with them and be their God.'"

—REVELATION 21:3

As followers of God, we tend to think about heaven a lot. It's one of God's coolest, best promises to his people—that we will one day get to join him there. And there's a lot of mystery surrounding the particulars of heaven. What's it really like? How will we feel when we get there? Is God in heaven different than God on Earth?

God's presence truly is everywhere, but God's presence in heaven is special. Heaven is like the focus of God's presence of blessing and glory. Unlike Earth, heaven is filled with God's presence *and* has no sin. Perhaps that's why God's blessing and glory is especially apparent in heaven.

Want to know something really wild? In Revelation, God says he will bring the New Heaven down to New Earth. That pure presence of God, unclouded by sin, will fill his renewed creation. Wow! It's mind-boggling to even think about it. But it's something we have to look forward to—another of God's excellent promises.

DAY 365

"Then I heard what sounded like a great multitude, like the roar of rushing waters and like loud peals of thunder, shouting: 'Hallelujah! For our Lord God Almighty reigns.'"

—REVELATION 19:6

Hallelujah! Maybe you've never said that word aloud, but if you've spent much time in church, you've probably at least heard it. It's a Hebrew word that's an exclamation of praise—a shout of adoration. We say "hallelujah" to express our worship of the God we adore.

But the truth is, we're able to adore him because we were first adored *by* him. We are God's precious daughters. We've seen through our own experiences and his Word many proofs of his deep love for us.

How can we better show God our appreciation? Are there areas in your life you'd like to begin working on? Would you like to grow in prayer, Bible study, or service to others? Pick one or two areas you'd like to focus on, and get to work. God is with you—enabling you, strengthening you, and adoring you.

NIV Holy Bible for Girls, Journal Edition

The *NIV Holy Bible for Girls, Journal Edition* is the perfect way to apply Scripture to your everyday life. Designed with the thoughtful writer in mind, a whimsical cover and journaling lines inspire reflection in God's Word. This Bible contains the full text of the best-selling New International Version (NIV) translation.

Features include:

- Lines on each page for journaling and notes
- Thick paper perfect for any writing utensil
- A presentation page for gift giving
- A "How to Use This Bible" page to get started on the right foot
- Ribbon marker
- The complete text of the bestselling New International Version (NIV)

Hardcover (turquoise): 9780310758969
Hardcover (pink): 9780310759065
Hardcover (purple): 9780310759652
Hardcover (mint): 9780310759805

Available in stores and online!